LIFE
CAN
BE
SEXUAL

ELMER N. WITT

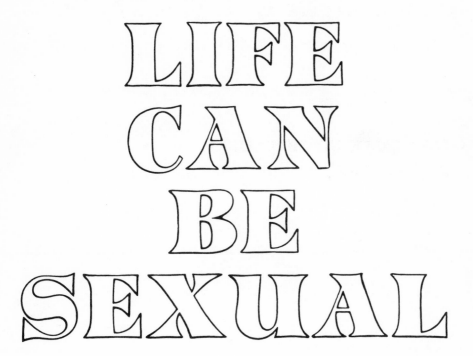

LIFE CAN BE SEXUAL

CONCORDIA PUBLISHING HOUSE

ACKNOWLEDGEMENTS

The author gratefully acknowledges permission by the publishers to quote from the following copyrighted material:

Association Press, New York, N. Y.: J. C. Wynn, ed., *Sex, Family, and Society,* 1966.

Division of Youth Activity, The American Lutheran Church, Minneapolis, Minn.: Ewald Bash, *Love and Sexuality: A Place to Walk,* 1966.

CONCORDIA SEX EDUCATION SERIES

W. J. Fields, D. D., Editor

Life Can Be Sexual
© Copyright 1967
   Elmer N. Witt
   Chicago, Illinois
   All Rights Reserved

Concordia Publishing House, St. Louis, Missouri
Concordia Publishing House Ltd., London, E. C. 1
Library of Congress Catalog Card No. 67-24880
MANUFACTURED IN THE UNITED STATES OF AMERICA

DEDICATION

With fondness to . . .   *dedication*
Grace, Marge, Carol, Diane, Selda,
Elizabeth, Miriam, Nancy, Kitty, Barbara, Patricia, Esther, Lois, Donna,
JoAnn, Dorothy, Leone, Gladys, Catherine, Winnie, Mary, Judy, Elaine,
Ilene, Lucille, Ann, Janet, Helene, Betty, Joan, Sabra, Wilma,
Joyce, Thea, Corinne, Vernette, Norma, Signe, Thelda, Kathy, Hilde,
Rosemarie, Jeri, Jeanne, Mariane, Shelby, Renata, Carline, Fern, Lydia,
Loraine, Alice, Pauline, Karen, Linda, Jolan, Joellyn, Ardis, Ruth,
Bonnie, Dorcas, Jackie, Lucy, Priscilla, Margaret, Kim, Marcia, Susan, Jurine,
Helen, Connie, Christine, Caroline, Maryann, Madelyn, Doris

I also thank my wife, *Virginia,*
for typing copies of the manuscript.

GOD
WHO
on many occasions
and in a variety of ways
SPOKE
in times past
to the fathers
BY THE PROPHETS

HAS
in these last days
SPOKEN
to us
BY
HIS
SON

. . . And I am glad

contents

a case of honesty

A CASE OF HONESTY

This is more than a sex-education manual!

In other words, it does more than give a lot of information about the reproduction process. This information is important and some of it is included here. But there are lots of good books that go into this process in more detail.

This is a book on how to think about sex and sexuality. And it's a book written unashamedly from a Christian perspective. It's an effort to translate—in terms, phrases, and style that I hope you catch on to—just what God has in mind for you as a Christian, sexual human being.

I think He has lots in mind. And I feel it's worthwhile to share what I think some of it is.

But . . . writing a book is no fun. Especially one about sexuality. It's almost pure blood, sweat, tears, and procrastination. I'm glad I wrote it, however. And I'm glad it's finished. It may help you understand what I've written if I take time to tell you why it got to be such a struggle.

First, I was and am afraid. A friend talked me into writing this. He's still a friend, but I should have realized how "hot" a subject sexuality is in anybody's judgment. To try to lay it on the line honestly, or, as it has turned out, to try to lay myself on the line openly, is asking for trouble.

Second, sexuality is a tough enough subject to tackle on a one-to-one basis with people you know. I now know how difficult it is to try to write helpfully about this very personal topic to a mass of unlocated, unknown, and unnumbered students, of whom you are an important part.

If you are now properly sympathetic, may I try to say in as easy as a-b-c sentences what I did to make the burden of writing halfway light:

a. I assumed your willingness to start from scratch and talk about sexuality as if it were a brand-new discovery or a contemporary revelation. I'm quite convinced it isn't, as the 63 books and 22 magazines I l ought testify. But starting from scratch is easier; at least at the outset we know where each other is.

b. I listed many of the important words used most frequently on this subject and then made up, copied, or adapted definitions for use on these pages. These are listed on pages 103 – 105 at the back of the book. Checking these definitions may help us get across to each other.

c. To keep the book from looking like a glorified typing-class exercise, I tried to keep the chapters and paragraphs short and to make certain ideas stand out by different type patterns. As an extra, possibly for discussion purposes, I gathered the "special illustrations" in Chapter 9. Since these are "borrowed" from others, I think you'll enjoy the change of pace (they may be the best part of the book).

d. I determined not to pretend to be anything but a 43-year-old, male, church professional, married, with five children. My beautiful thatch of hair is long departed, so I can't even make it as a guitar-carrying folk singer. I've tried to accept you in the middle of that unlocated, unknown, and unnumbered mass of youth out there. I ask you to accept me, with accumulating years, not too much experience, but plenty of willingness, at this faithful typewriter on a dining room table stacked with books.

e. I resolved to be as honest as possible. I tried to say what I think. What I don't personally believe, you won't find in these pages. That may have put some crimps in the content, but perhaps it helped the style.

f. Finally, I have taken for granted that you are willing – maybe not eager, but willing – to think. Youth are supposed to be professional thinkers. At least that's what I believe education, inside or outside a classroom, is all about. God's gift of your mind in reasonably good working condition is also His invitation for you to "learn" about sexuality.

Blessings . . .

PENTECOST, 1967

sex is

being

36-24-36

SEX IS BEING 36-24-36

SEX is being 36-24-36.

SEXUALITY is knowing the meaning and power of being 36-24-36.

CHRISTIANITY clues us about where sexuality — with all its meaning and power — comes from and why.

And it clues us to do something about it!

That's the message of this book in a nutshell.

And the main line is:

"to do something about it!"

This approach assumes that Christiantity is about "doing." What we *do* is proof of what we *are*.

That's the hint we get at the beginning of God's contact with man. The Scriptures start with God, who "proves" who He *is* by what He *does*. It doesn't lead off with a huge discussion or argument about God. Or where He comes from. Or why.

He just "is."

And because He "is," He does: He thinks, decides, speaks, acts, creates, evaluates, rests.

We know God through what He has done and still does, including what He's done to give us the Word about His love for us.

> So people who are aware of God and His love — let's call them Christians — are people who do things because they "are." They are people made alive to the possibilities God has provided. Sounds simple, doesn't it? Maybe *too* simple. But it's true.

Some books specialize in biological and psychological information about sex. That's good. Others stress what not to do. That's good. Still others look at sex mainly from the view of dating, courtship, and marriage. And that's good. The goal of this book is to point up the Christian understanding of being sexual and to help young people *do something about it.*

And a book like this can be written, in fact had to be written, because of what sex and sexuality and Christianity are all about.

To get started, we will take apart the three ideas at the start of this chapter from a couple of points of view and then try quickly and helpfully to put them back together again. The point to remember from the outset is: all three ideas belong together. Taking them apart to examine them is artificial; life isn't that neat. And it happens in books only because till now ideas and words moving between people don't work any other way.

So let's start the taking-apart process.

SEX

We began with: SEX IS BEING 36-24-36. Now that's not entirely true. But it's partially true and true enough to be of help at this point.

It's true because it says that "sex" has something to do with the body. In our part of the world at least, the shape of a girl or woman, especially her bust, is a formidable symbol of sex. People call 36-24-36 women "sexy" because they have some obvious equipment for what is popularly called "sex." And that's partially true: sex involves the body. But the whole story of "sex" is much, much more complicated.

14

We are all born man or woman; each of us has an identifiable sexual nature. After finding out if a newborn baby is healthy, the first thing a parent wants to know: Is it a girl or a boy? In one sense, sex is primarily a matter of our anatomical and physiological structure, the way we're built and the sex organs we come with. The specialized physical parts of the male and female make possible the reproduction of species, in our case, having human babies. But physical equipment does not exhaust the meaning of human sex.

In addition to the special parts of the body of man and woman, everyone is born with a sex urge. It's a basic element of human nature. Sometimes we call it "sex attraction." It's a "reaching out of the spirit through the body." It's physical in the sense that our hormones, etc., are involved. But sex attraction cannot be put under a microscope. It's more than meets the eye or the touch. It includes awareness of the attractiveness of another person, the tone of a voice, the memory of an experience, the dream of the future. It's what Emmy Lou of the cartoon means when she says, "What I like about Alvin is, he's a boy."

Along with the parts of the body designed for reproduction, the sex urge is part of our human nature. To care about someone and have someone care about us is our deepest human need. This need is at work in all our contacts with other human beings. We have the physical and emotional capacities to love and to receive love. There are intricacies and problems involved. But don't rush. We'll get to them later. At this point we want to pin down the fact that sexuality has deeper meaning than simply being or seeing someone who is 36-24-36.

SEXUALITY

Take a look at the next statement: SEXUALITY IS KNOWING THE MEANING AND POWER OF BEING 36-24-36.

For our own purposes we are using the word "sexuality" to mean something more than "sex." Understanding sex means being aware of the body and the physical responses between persons because of their bodies. Sexuality means going beyond the physical-emotional process to discover what sex means in the total life of a person and society.

We are sexual beings not only when at certain times we experience specific sexual desires; rather we are sexual beings in all that we are and all that we do. Sexuality means understanding sex as an expression of the human personality.

We can also talk about sexuality in terms of our femaleness and maleness (see "Definitions" on page 103). When we do, we again mean more than the reproductive organs and more than the so-called feminine and masculine traits, such as physical strength, esthetic appreciation, interest in cooking, preference for the out-of-doors, providing financial security, sensitivity to feelings, etc. Many of these distinctions are superficial. Some are more cultural than sexual. Female and male are different. This meaning of femaleness and maleness for all of life's relationships is what we mean by sexuality.

Sexuality emphasizes the every-day-ness and every-place-ness of sex. It cannot be isolated from our humanness. It is not something we turn on and off like a faucet. Nor is it simply something we learn to do, like driving a car or playing tennis. Sexuality is an avenue of personal expression, an important way of letting people know who you are, what you're like, and how you feel and think. It's an expression of our humanity that we can learn to know and direct.

Information on reproduction, or "how to have babies," is not sex education. It doesn't get at the full meaning of sexuality. Far from it. We know a good deal about *reproductive* education, but we are just beginning to learn what being a man or a woman means, about how people use sexual powers for each other or against each other. Most people have long recognized the power of sex. Leaders in education, government, science, and religion are only now beginning to recognize the importance of sexuality—the way sex invades and influences all of life—and what can be done about it.

Looked at objectively (as if we could!), sexuality in itself is good. Actually it's simply a fact of nature, a force of immeasurable power. And at the same time it's complicated. It offers pleasure and power, makes us feel good or bad. It frightens us and intrigues us. But sexuality isn't God. It's a real-life fact about being human.

Ever since we were small we've been tempted to like "gifts" more than the "Giver." Getting to be mature includes getting a better understanding of the Giver through His gifts.

Sexuality is a gift. Not only because "it's God's idea in the first place." That's true.

But there's more to it than its origin. According to God's own wisdom and design, our sexuality is given as a stepping-stone toward understanding our relationship to Him. And therefore to life itself, with people, right now.

That's a mouthful. It's what we meant when we said: CHRISTIANITY CLUES US ABOUT WHERE SEXUALITY—WITH ALL ITS MEANING AND POWER—COMES FROM, AND WHY.

That's what the next chapter is all about.

TO LIVE IS TO LOVE

There's no "recipe" for relationships, like:

Take a generous share of girl, stir in a quiet beach, add one full boy, mix thoroughly and garnish lightly with guitar, to produce a "they lived happily ever after" relationship.

Nor can you put it into a mathematical formula:

$$\textbf{G (girl) + B (boy) + 2C (car and cash)} = \textbf{X}^{\textbf{c}} \textbf{(ecstasy)}$$

Nor can you put it in terms of a football diagram:

P (parents)
o o o o o o
X X X X X
Y (youth)

Although all three of these illustrations talk about relationships. Relationships are what life is made up of. They are our connections, our associations, our involvement with human beings. They are one sign of being alive. Being alive is more than breathing regularly or keeping our heart pumping at a satisfactory rate. All of us know people who do that and still seem "dead." At times we feel "dead on our feet." And usually that means *not* being able to respond to whatever's going on around us. One definition of being alive is to be awake, to be aware, to notice people, things and events, to respond to what's happening.

And a huge dimension of what's happening in the life of each of us is "relationships." We're surrounded by them. We really live through them. They begin with the first relationship to Mom before, during, and after birth. And then to Dad. Then relatives, neighbors, and friends. In a short time our lives are filled with relationships. Many seem the same, but each is distinct. Some are short and casual; others go on for years. Some are intimate, others formal. We expect a different relationship with the first-hour English teacher than with the good-looking fellow or gal in the next block. A large variety of relationships in this rich world of ours are part of being human.

The advantage and disadvantage of human relationships is that they are personal. Because they are personal, deep and lasting relationships can be made. A fellow meets a girl. They click. A long friendship develops. That's an advantage. But because relationships are personal, they also are unpredictable. They can't be readily "controlled." They aren't consistent or constant. Another fellow meets a girl. They click. Later they break up. They get together again. They break up again. And neither of them necessarily knows why. That's a disadvantage. Or at least it keeps us guessing about relationships.

Not a great deal of argument about this. The tough job is how to make this next part not sound merely like a "pitch."

HE STARTED IT

The clue about relationships — and therefore about sexuality — comes from God. He started it all: sexuality and relationships. This is true not only in terms of His work as our Creator. It's true in terms of His own relationship with us. God makes Himself known as personal. He thinks; He wants; He decides; He acts; He communicates.

God is so personal that the Scriptures say He is Love. That's a description of Him in terms of relationship, the way He wants to be related to man. God knows us, sees our struggle with relationships, hears our cry for help with our sexuality, and is keenly aware of our separation from Him and from each other, which makes relationships tough.

And because God is love, He went into action. God delivered us. We call this action of God "redemption." Simply put, this means that God in Jesus Christ restored to us and to all creation our original value and purpose.

Through Christ we are related to God. To "have faith" in God means to "have connections" with God. Real "knowledge" of God depends on our "union" or connection with God's action for us in Christ, with His death and resurrection. This connection is not merely accepting some truths as historical or some doctrine as accurate. Christian faith is a direct contact, a living relationship between us and the Spirit of the risen Christ. For God, to speak is to act. His Word is power. And through His Word He reaches out to touch and stir the center of our own being and gives us the new life of Christ in our own lives.

The Bible calls this God's way of "making us alive again." In other words, God in Christ wakes us up, makes us aware, able to notice people, things, and events, makes us able to respond to what's happening in the world around us. Christians see, hear, and think about the same kinds of things as others do. High school hours are just as long. Families talk or don't talk much the same way. The difference is that Christians recognize and acknowledge God at work in all of life with His judgment and grace.

Through Christ we get to live "on purpose" for others — other kids, our teachers, our parents. Through Christ we get to put God's value on people as they are and where they are — male, female, young, old, even those who are tough to know or like. Through Christ we build personal relationships with others on the basis of love, in terms of what we can do for them rather than what we want from them.

CHRISTIANITY AND SEXUALITY

Here endeth "the pitch." — Now what does all this mean for our sexuality? Earlier we made the point that sexuality means the understanding of sex as an expression of the human personality. It's a way of letting people know through your whole self just who you are, what you're like, and how you feel and think. We express our sexuality through relationships — girls with fellows, fellows with girls, with our parents, and, of course, with members of the same sex. Whenever we express our personality to someone else, we are expressing our sexuality whether we are aware of this or not.

Here are seven direct applications of Christianity to sexuality:
1. As Christians we see sexuality as a God-given and God-redeemed way of relating to people. Christ redeemed our total

being: body, soul, mind, emotions, and desires. He rules over earthly matter and human processes, including our sexual relationships.

2. As Christians our understanding of sexuality begins with our view of our own selves, the value we place on ourselves as persons for whom Christ died and in whom God lives. Usually our acceptance of others depends on our acceptance of ourselves.

3. As Christians we recognize the sexual dimension of all our relationships with others and work at seeing all persons in God's perspective. We learn that "what happens to persons is what counts." To love means to seek the best for others in our relationships with them.

4. As Christians we affirm the spontaneity of our sexuality. Our relationships are free rather than forced. They happen. "A tree bears flowers and fruit without instruction or command." To love means to be free to respond. God's love frees our sexuality to bring about His kind of love in the everyday, extraordinary, frustrating, exciting situations of life.

5. As Christians we take seriously God's particular concerns, directions, and limitations for expressing our sexuality. This especially involves sexual intercourse, marriage, and the reproduction of children.

6. As Christians we affirm the joy of God's forgiveness for our misuse of sexuality. We are aware of our neglect to love as fully as we are able. We know we often twist our sexuality from love into lust. But God conquered lust and paid the price for sin. In His Son we are made alive again sexually.

7. As Christians we recognize God as the source of practical, personal power to guide and control our sexuality. The promise of His Spirit as the "One to stand with us" is constant and clear. What God makes, He services.

A recap of what we've said so far: In chapter one we pointed up that sexuality is more than just knowing about sexual functions and drives. It's the way our whole being expresses itself to someone else in a way in which each is changed.

In this chapter we emphasized that sexuality expresses itself through relationships . . . that we're head over heels in relationships, most of them beyond our ability to direct or control . . . that God gives us the clue to healthy relationships through His relationship to us in Jesus Christ . . . and, therefore, that our sexual relationships have a lot to do with God.

Next up: specifics on the extra-special sexual relationship of having babies.

the reproductive record

THE REPRODUCTIVE RECORD

Here's where we get to the birds and the bees and the flowers.

Be sure to let your parents read this chapter. It's quite clear that parents are not always as informed about matters sexual as they want to be or we expect them to be. *Look* magazine said it bluntly: "Behind each [sexually] ignorant teen-ager is usually a shy or ignorant parent."

Be sure they read the whole chapter. But before we begin spinning the reproductive record, we pause for a brief message from our Sponsor:

This year, bodies are in! And I don't mean bodies by Fisher! I mean human bodies—yours, mine. Actually, bodies have always been "in," but lately "Anti-Bodies" have been promoting their "hate bodies" campaign. Maintaining that it's wrong to like yourself, they imply that the human body may be the source of all our problems with sexuality. Frightened and uninformed persons, and not only little old ladies from Pasadena, have been taken in by this insidious attack.

But bodies are good. I'm sure you would never want to be without one. Bodies are popular. Some of my best friends have bodies. Bodies are useful. In the midst of a national housing shortage, bodies are housing people throughout the length and breadth of the land.

So, remember your bodies, and keep these three simple statements in mind:

First, *when God came into the world, He chose to do so by assuming a body. What's good enough for Him is good enough for you.*

Second, *redemption took place through the body of Christ.*

chapter

3

Flesh and blood are redeemed through flesh and blood. Christ lived, suffered, and died for the whole person. And so restored the whole person—with spiritual, social, intellectual, emotional, and physical dimensions—to the original value and purpose of God. His love makes our body, with all its complex and perplexing functions, a temple of the Holy Spirit.

*And **third,** the body will share in the Resurrection. The body is the Lord's, in this life and in that to come.*

So get in the swim! Love God with all you are: body, heart, soul, strength, mind; and love your whole *neighbor as you love your whole self.*

And now the reproductive record.

Most of us know less about the human reproductive process than we realize or are willing to admit.

Our particular stance as Christians leans on this basic information but sees broader and deeper meaning for the birth process. Our starting point is God and creation. God involves man in creation. He gives us powers through which we express ourselves as men, as women. He equips us with power to "create" relationships. He gives the power of decision, the choice between now and later, between green and blue, between good and evil.

God furnishes us the power to communicate, to reach out and make real contact as sexual beings with other sexual beings in ways that change both. This is more than speech or words. "Communicating" with another individual might include a smile, friendship, acceptance, preference, a handshake, a kiss, obedience, an embrace, leadership, intercourse, art, silence, music, and much more.

So sexuality doesn't exist for itself or by itself. It is a rich and needed part of our development as persons. We behave as we do because we are male or female. Our creation in God's image is supernatural. Our sexuality is natural, part of being human. We use it for either good or bad. It's an expression of our humanity that we can learn to know and direct.

AN INSIDE JOB

The place and direction of our lives as created sexual beings is *within* us. Sexual knowledge is different *in kind* from knowledge about sex. Sexual knowledge is knowing ourselves and others "from the inside." Through His "inside Man," the Holy Spirit, God provides the inside means for understanding and directing sexuality, including the sexual processes of our bodies.

Besides, we need to understand the sexual processes, like other bodily functions, in order to have good health and a satisfying life. Most aspects of health are considered "personal" matters. Sex functioning differs from our other physical functions in that while it is considered the most private and personal process of the human body, it is meant to involve another person. So we must understand not only our own sex nature but that of the other sex also, and the relation of one to the other.

To begin with, the development of our sexual processes is perfectly natural. It happens automatically. Our bodies mature and the sex organs develop and begin to function.

God gave nature many ways of being "intelligent." For example, in the human body there's a kind of "chemical intelligence" in the sperm and egg cells that come together to make a new person. This "intelligence" stays in each cell of the body throughout life, directing its growth.

There is another kind of "chemical intelligence" in the ductless (endocrine) glands—the pituitary, the thyroid, the adrenal, the testes, and the ovaries (don't you wish you would have stayed awake in Freshman Biology?). Each of these glands produces hormones. Each responds in some way to the hormones of the other. Together they help keep a person's emotional life in balance with his life of thought and action.

INTRICATE FEMALE

The female reproductive system operates on one of nature's intricate timepieces, the ovarian rhythm. This (usually) 28-day menstrual cycle begins at puberty and continues until the childbearing years are past. Normally this cycle is interrupted only by pregnancy. Menstruation is just one of the sequences of events in this cycle.

Actually the menstrual cycle begins in a woman when an egg ripens and leaves the ovary (ovulation) and moves through the Fallopian tube toward the uterus (womb). In order for an egg united with a sperm cell to take hold in the uterus, the lining of the uterus must be a new, fresh tissue. This freshness cannot be maintained continuously. If an egg is not fertilized within about 48 hours after its release from the ovary, it dies and begins to disintegrate. The old lining tissue also breaks down and is passed out of the uterus to be replaced by a new one. This is called "menstruation." The old tissue has many blood cells in it, and so menstruation normally involves bleeding. After 3 to 5 days the uterus begins to return to its previous state.

INCREDIBLE MALE

The male reproductive system maintains a constant supply of sperm cells in incredible numbers. These are stored, ready for use, from the time of sexual maturity (puberty) on through life. There is no cycle; they're always there.

If after sexual intercourse (coitus) a sperm cell makes its way to the egg at the proper time and unites with it (fertilization, or pregnancy), the menstrual cycle comes to a halt. The amazing provisions of a woman's body for the 9-month nurture of the egg are triggered into action. An ovarian rhythm is not resumed until sometime after the birth of the child.

Obviously this is only a simplified description of a biological process you have more than likely seen in films or have read about before. What we bypassed for the moment was that as the testes of the male produce sperm cells which accumulate as semen, they create a kind of hunger for outlet. The real hunger, male and female, comes from hormones secreted into the bloodstream from testes and ovaries.

These are a new kind of "chemical intelligence." They provide a new outlook on life, a desire for sexual satisfaction that must be dealt with personally. This hunger for sexual outlet develops individually. There's no timetable or barometer to check. The signals are obvious, however: interest in the opposite sex increases sharply, physical responses are stronger and come more rapidly, the desire to touch is intensified.

Trying to live a balanced life is never easy. And it is not made any easier by having new physical capacities, new emotional energies, and new responsibilities to deal with all at once. This is what usually happens at the time of sexual maturity. Each of us has to face it individually, without previous personal experience. It's a little like taking a semester final test when you haven't been in the course.

Some people would naturally like to duck this responsibility of handling sexual hunger. For comfort and reassurance in a frightening situation they try to take the easy way out by plunging into sexual intercourse and even into marriage. This might work *if* the only purpose of sexual maturity were to get a sperm cell and an egg cell together. But that's not what maturing experiences in sexuality are really about. Such experiences are designed to open new avenues outside ourselves, new ways of being related to the world of persons, new ways of getting to know ourselves. And we don't find these ways when we seek quick comfort by avoiding personal and honest decisions about our newfound sexual abilities.

Bodies are "in" and the reproductive process is a reality of life. Along with it all we pick up the huge responsibility for control of some very explosive emotions. It's a power-packed situation that has contributed to the rise and fall of many persons as well as nations. Let's take a look at what all this body-built-in power has been doing for us lately.

picking up the tab

PICKING UP THE TAB

Christians need not mourn the passing of the "conspiracy of silence" about sex and sexuality. Once you get used to it, talking or writing about sex really isn't too difficult.

But if sex is so good and being sexual is so normal and even talking out loud about it can become easy, what's the furor all about? Why do so many people seem so edgy about sex?

Question: How come we are sexually uncomfortable — or uncomfortably sexual?

Answer: There's a massive, unmarked, peculiar, pervasive REVOLUTION going on!

Call it what you will — a major rethinking, upheaval, crisis, obsession, "sexplosion" — that's what's going on. S-E-X is everywhere. The U. S. A. is called a "sexual nuthouse," almost "the most sex-obsessed country in the world." In less than 30 years our culture has undergone drastic changes. In more than one way we have exchanged ankle-length dresses for bikinis.

As one "way out front" young person put it:

> The revolution will be far more than sexual. Repression as we now know it will go down the drain. People are going back to sex in loud rebellion against the sterility in our society. For all our freedom, we just cannot let go. But there will come a day. And it will be soon. And I assume that the church will again be out-to-lunch, probably discussing whether the symbolic motif in worship has anything to do with weight-lifting.

Is this the clamor of a cynic or the voice of one crying in the wilderness?

Some think the revolution is simply an effort (pretty effective) to tear down all the "Danger — High Tension Wire" signs around sex.

Others say it's like wanting to distribute neutrons and plutonium as toys for kids.

And still others, including Hugh Hefner, owner-editor of *Playboy* magazine, think this revolution is just an indication that we are growing up sexually and achieving a "healthy enjoyment of life in rejecting the restraints of the past."

A TAXING INHERITANCE

Whoever or whichever is true (we choose "sides" in the next chapter), one thing is more and more certain: it's youth who are picking up the tab. "Our era is distinguished from others by the absence of an agreed system of values. Today love wanders about, sick and feverish, without knowing where it belongs." And *young people* inherit the confusion. They reap the bitter harvest of silence and fear. Youth are the primary "victims" of a society which makes "wisdom in many areas — including sex — difficult to attain."

Reactions to such observations are as varied as they are predictable. Take your pick:

"Oh, it's always been that way."
"I couldn't agree more. And what's worse, there isn't a thing anyone can do about it."
"Now just don't get so excited. It'll all work out all right in the end; it always has."
"I told you so!"
"Don't bother me now; I'm busy."
"Well, it may be true for some, but it sure isn't true about the people I know."

Not to mention, of course, its all being "part of a communist (or fascist?) plot" to undermine our morals, or the result of radioactive fallout from atomic bombs affecting our sexual makeup.

None of these is helpful. But if it's true that, like it or not, youth are marked for picking up the tab, you're at least entitled to know a little more of what the revolution is all about. There are competent studies of varying depth listed in the bibliography. Our goal here is to demonstrate that this revolution is not fantasy nor rigged to work out all right in the end. The revolution is for real, for life, and for right now.

EXPERTS

To touch some of the more important bases, let me introduce you to a few persons who have something worthwhile to say about this revolution. These excerpts from their writings get at the nature, scope, implications, depth, and some specifics of the "massive revolution" we're living in. Obviously, quoting these experts by no means endorses all they say, here or elsewhere. Some of the quotes dig deeper than others. Parts of them may sail right over your head. Read them twice if you have to. They're worth knowing about. And anyway, every book is entitled to one tough chapter.

First, meet "Mr. American Sex Revolution" himself, Pitirim A. Sorokin. Already in 1954 he was ridiculing "the big change" going on in words like these:

> The sex drive is now declared to be the most vital mainspring of human behavior. In the name of science, its fullest satisfaction is urged as a necessary condition of man's health and happiness. Sex inhibitions are viewed as the main source of frustrations, mental and physical illness and criminality. Sexual chastity is ridiculed as a prudish superstition. . . . Sexual profligacy and prowess are proudly glamorized. *Homo sapiens* is replaced by *homo sexualis*. . . . The traditional "child of God" created in God's image is turned into a sexual apparatus powered by sex instinct, preoccupied with sex matters, aspiring for, and dreaming and thinking mainly of, sex relations.[1]

You can often tell the significance of an issue by the status of the journalists writing about it. Here's a description of the scope of the revolution's impact by one of *Look* magazine's senior editors, Leonard Gross:

> Yet, for all the breakaway from Victorian morality, the amount of sexual ignorance remains about the same. Studies indicate that almost 17 per cent of all brides, at least one third of high-school brides, are pregnant as they march

down the aisle. . . . In 1964 alone, girls of high-school age aborted 180,000 pregnancies. Reported cases of syphilis among teen-agers have more than tripled since 1956; young people under 20 account for more than one in five cases of venereal disease. . . . For each child physically scarred by sex, there are thousands for whom it is no more than a toy, a game, a shallow, selfish quest.[2]

Harvey Cox of the Harvard Divinity School faculty describes some implications he sees in the revolution:

> Sex has become one of those things, like brushing your teeth, taking a brisk walk, and having a satisfying hobby, which have their place in the well-rounded life — after marriage. The models who appear in these young married women's and family magazines are agressively healthy and happy. Their sexual allure is that of a bouncy high school cheerleader who has aged 15 years. One feels that something very important to sexuality is lost in this rendition. Just as in the Playboy perspective, sex is trivialized by being reduced to recreation. *The potency and power of sex, its highly charged capacity to jar everything else in life is somehow overlooked.* Young couples, and aging ones too, find held before them for emulation a kind of happy asexual sexuality that flows but never rages, an emasculated sex which never threatens to overrun its boundaries.[3]

The revolution is not exclusively American. In his book *Honest to God,* as well as in *Christian Morals Today,* Bishop John A. T. Robinson of Great Britain desperately seeks to get the church to face squarely the "new morality" confronting youth today. Here's a sample:

> "Dread of being a social outcast is the main reason why teenagers have sexual intercourse before marriage," writes a girl student. . . .
>
> I want a morality which frees people from that. But I know we shall not get it by simply saying 'Thou shalt not!'

a bit louder. Young people today ask 'why?' They want a basis for morality that makes sense in terms of personal relationships. They want *honesty* in sex, as in everything else. And that is what chastity is — inside marriage or out of it. It is not just abstinence. I believe that most young people are genuinely looking for a morality that cuts deeper, is more searching and less superficial than the ready-made rules of their parents.[4]

The last quotation affirms the ecumenical spirit of the sexual revolution. A Roman Catholic, Richard A. McCormick, S. J., feels sex is becoming a mechanized, manipulatable, tabulated, microscoped "thing" always on call.

> Actually, the basic ingredient of the Puritan outlook was and is fear. This fear assumes different masquerades. At one time it will take the form of reticence. At another it is a noisy and gawdy exhibitionism. At still another an uneasy preoccupation posing as casualness. Because modern man is progressively incapable of recognizing value in sexuality and coping with it in the real world, of taking it seriously, he shows that he is deathly afraid of the genuine article. Of course he will hide this fear, even from himself. But it is there. All his protestations notwithstanding (indeed, precisely because of them) Mr. Hefner is above all the polished symbol of this deep fear, hence of this Puritanism.[5]

That's a sample of what some folks say is going on. What's happening is not organized. And never easy to understand. But it's a first-class rebellion. About the only thing these excerpts missed is the recognition of many more kinds and degrees of "mixed-up" sexual activities, such as pornography, masturbation, homosexuality, sodomy, transvestism, mate-swapping, etc.

You can tell from their comments that some of these writers seem more at ease with the revolution than others. As usual, there are two sides to the story. On the one hand, the sexual revolt was inevitable.

As our huge world and little worlds have been urbanized, technical-ized, and secularized, the values of persons and things were bound to be hit. They couldn't escape. Things aren't the same. People aren't the same. Life isn't the same. Something had to give.

On the other hand, revolution is a tricky business. Who chooses the sides, draws the lines, determines the terms for restoration of peace? Tradition can't be all wrong any more than contemporary ideas can be all right. And vice versa.

The sorriest part was pinpointed by our youthful "out-fronter" above with the line: "And I assume that the church will again be out-to-lunch. . . ." That hurts our pride as members of the church. And maybe it should. Because for the most part it's true. It isn't easy to be out-to-lunch during a revolution, especially when you're living right in the middle of it and really are part of it.

But that's what we've been doing.

And we're all paying a price. But I'm afraid what the man said is true: *You* are the fall guy. *Youth* is slated for picking up the tab. *You're* being asked to "come alive" sexually in a time of

> . . . increased confusion about what's morally right or wrong;
>
> . . . less conviction about *how to decide* what's morally right or wrong;
>
> . . . greater need to "psych out" or rationalize difficult moral decisions;
>
> . . . massive and often undetected influence from movies, pop songs, TV, magazines, and books for setting moral standards;
>
> . . . increasingly effective and attractive portrayal of the "possibilities" of sex without commitment;
>
> . . . increased lack of clarity on what marriage is all about.

For youth on the road to maturity, all this adds up to some pretty inevitable struggles with some mighty hazardous powers.

power
struggle

POWER STRUGGLE

The best information indicates you cannot get insurance for or against sexuality. Even if you could, the policy probably wouldn't apply during these uncertain days of revolution. So we're going to have to figure out some other protection plan for this dynamic force in human beings which we call sexuality.

"Dynamic" and "force" are popular words in today's newspapers, magazines, and books. They're used a lot in advertising. They're related to the "power" family of words like energy, potency, vitality and have special appeal for those who think young. These are words of life itself.

From the moment we are born, we are involved in power and power relationships. It's simply part of being in the world. All relationships, even the most personal ones between parents and children or fellows and girls, involve the use and adjustment, the give and take, of power.

In the last couple of decades "power" has taken on new meaning. Through nuclear fission we know more power than has ever been known before. Through the increased study of man and society we have come to recognize the widespread *kinds* of power that surround and influence us. Some are obvious; others are strictly under the counter or behind the scenes.

For instance, the impersonal "rulers" of our society are really powers: economy, mass media, public opinion, nationalism, religious sentiments, racial prejudice, moral rules, philosophies of life, etc. Sex is one of these constantly-present, instantly-on-call, persistently-at-work powers.

As Christians we quickly affirm that "power belongs to God." The powers listed above are not evil. They are not created by the devil, who cannot create anyway, but by God Himself. They are powers meant to be the skeleton of the different worlds we live in, a framework for our lives. Our daily existence doesn't consist simply of logical reactions to our own desires and wishes. Nor is it the clear combination of the success our work deserves and the punishment our mistakes bring us.

Life is not that simple. It's ten times more complicated! The powers at work in our lives are tough to spot and even tougher to handle.

But let's be particular: all the "powers" we can list or think of, whatever they may be, were created by and for Jesus Christ.

This is the annoying particularity the New Testament is filled with. St. Paul wrote about "powers" frequently. In the first chapter of Colossians he makes clear that Jesus Christ is the focal point of all powers. "All things are held together in Him." The Greek word he used has the same root as our word "system." Paul says that Christ is "the System of creation." For Him and by Him all things were created.

Including the power of sex.

That's not only interesting, that's basic.

DOUBLE-EDGED POWERS

The powers we mentioned were created by God as friendly agents, useful instruments, ready servants of God and man. But like men, the powers have become separated from God and so miss their calling to be servants. Like men, they're double-edged; they cut in either direction. They're a mixture of evil and good, each fighting for control.

This was seen most clearly in the life of Christ. When God became man, the powers set out to kill Him. Their real hostility to God came out into the open. It seems that all the powers of the earth—religious, political, emotional, physical—were assembled to kill Jesus.

The Christian faith is that Jesus Christ conquered the powers. He "led them as captives in His triumphal procession." He was "made a curse for us." The sinless One became sin in our behalf. He was abandoned by God. He actually died. The cross was the sign of His defeat and at the same time the sign of His victory. For Christ rose again, and in His resurrection He triumphed over the evil powers that attacked Him, the same powers that kept man away from God. These powers are now forced to see that Jesus carried away the sin of the world.

The victory has been won, but the effects still have to be made visible. We are called to join Christ in His power struggle, not thinking of all those powers as our enemies but recognizing them as runaway horses that must be controlled. Through Christ's victory they can be reharnessed.

Let's corral the double-edged power of sex. God created this power as the servant of man and Himself. Through it He made possible satisfying relationship, personal joy, the excitement of reproduction, participation in His own process of creation.

DISTORTED IMAGES

But evil has given it a second face. Sex has become a god and enslaved all-too-willing men. We now are suddenly surrounded by negative commandments rather than freedom to deal positively with the powers God has given.

The distorted images of sex must be unmasked. Sex is a fully human activity originated by God. The evil at work within and among us tries to dehumanize it, to make it subhuman, to change God's gracious intent and determined desire. Here are some of its most popular and current distortions:

> *a merchandising technique*—the brassy misuse of sexual stimulation in selling, often to youth, within an economic system that seems increasingly to require a perversion of sexuality in order to survive;
>
> *a means to popularity*—the disastrous use of "what you've got" as escape from failure in the highly competitive "games" of dating;
>
> *a weapon for rebelling against parents*—hitting the folks over the head with the gift they have given us;
>
> *a recreational pursuit*—using sex for exercise or sport, without understanding or respect for its highly charged capacity to jar everything in life;
>
> *a social ladder*—collecting sexual trophies as membership dues with the "in" group;

a way to snag a mate — grabbing whomever we can, right now, for fear of missing matrimony;

a devotional act — worshiping the gift rather than the Giver, or scotch-taping specialized "spiritual" significance to man's "bodily" activity.

There is no stronger tie than the sexual one and no stronger destructive power than sexual power. For a younger generation the question of mastering life is always closely related to mastering the power of sex. We are told that in Germany some call it the "royal test of education."

This is not a textbook exam or theoretical test. The sexual struggle takes place in warm flesh and blood. It happens every day for most people. It can be subtle. It can be obvious. It varies in degree of intensity. It has many forms. Masturbation and homosexuality are two of the more widely experienced patterns of the sexual struggle for adolescents.

SELF

Masturbation is self-stimulation. "The experience — or at least the sensation — which we normally associate with sexual intercourse is in masturbation experienced with oneself. The sex organs are sensitive to rubbing, and the Latin root of the word 'masturbation' implies rubbing with one's hands." [6]

Still avoided as a subject by youth and by those whom they might consult, masturbation is surrounded with ignorance and fear. The consequences falsely attributed to masturbation are astonishing. These mistaken but popular beliefs have ranged from "stooping shoulders to damage to the genitals, and have included insanity, paralysis, acne, excess growth of hair, loss of hair, epilepsy, fatigue, impotence, stomach ulcers, insomnia, weak eyes, skin rashes and loss of weight." [7]

Now we laugh at these old threats, and rightly so. Masturbation by itself causes none of these things. But the pendulum is swinging to the other extreme. The impression is given that masturbation is not only normal but "good" for you.

But pendulum-swinging is dangerous. We have to take time to face some facts. One of these is that masturbation is sex turned in on ourselves. This is the reverse of what we have said about sexuality as an avenue of personal expression, the power to communicate, to reach out and make real contact as a sexual being with another sexual being in ways that change both. We have viewed it as part of our God-given power to "create relationships." Masturbation is centered on myself rather than on others. The more I concentrate on myself, the more I am cut off from others, and the less I am able to love.

And we know that masturbation can cause a great deal of guilt. Some of this grows out of twisted ideas about sex and very likely from the old wives' tales about masturbation. But some of it is very likely also due to turning inward, toward ourselves, that which was meant to turn us outward, toward others. Secrecy, loneliness, and fantasy, which accompany masturbation, often increase the sense of guilt. "The guilt in masturbation is also over the imagery of this accompanying fantasy, which may have all the unlimited possibilities of our vivid and erotic imagination. In masturbation, not only what we do is important, but what goes on in our minds as we do it." [8]

43

The masturbation complex is a most serious dimension of the struggle of sex turned in upon oneself. This takes place when masturbation is used as a means of escape when the going gets tough. The escape pattern digs its own rut. And the habit can easily fix a person's sexual attitude at a level on which others are manipulated in fantasy to serve his satisfaction. This can make "sexual communication" as we have described it almost impossible.

HOMOSEXUALITY

A discussion of homosexuality raises more passion and prejudice than almost any other subject except race. In both, fear and ignorance again are the basic enemies. The word "homosexuality" denotes a course of conduct as well as a "situation," or "condition." Homosexuality is the state of loving one's own sex rather than the opposite sex (heterosexuality). Studies indicate that people are not either homosexual or heterosexual. Most people are predominantly one or the other; most in fact are predominantly heterosexual.

There is both male and female homosexuality. Physical attraction and deep friendships are normal in early adolescent years. Scientific study of homosexuality is comparatively new and relatively unknown. It is *estimated* that about a third of all males have had some homosexual experience at some point. Homosexuality is generally considered less common among women.

Homosexual activity among younger males is usually promiscuous, that is, not limited to one other person. It usually takes place within the same age group and frequently finds physical expression in such acts as mutual masturbation.

It's easy to misunderstand the differences between homosexual "attraction" and homosexual "practice." Many young people experience homosexual attraction to people their own age as well as to older or younger people. A smaller number of young people actually "practice" homosexual acts over an extended period of time. The difference is important. Most of us cannot escape homosexual temptations, but homosexual practice usually involves choosing this pattern of action. In either situation the causes and contributing factors are usually complex. In both situations God in Christ reaches out to us with His judgment of what is wrong and, with His mercy, offers forgiveness and power.

Concerns to remember:

1. Our society is just beginning to study and to understand the phenomenon of homosexuality.
2. Most people who have early homosexual experiences grow up to live heterosexual lives.
3. Homosexuality *or* heterosexuality can be used simply to satisfy uncontrolled lust.
4. Although God made us to love all people, His design in nature and Scripture is clearly *for* heterosexuality and *against* homosexuality (see Romans 1). The standards of society and the law support this view.
5. The causes of homosexuality are complex. The best studies — and apparently there aren't many — by competent professionals

do not agree on basic sources of trouble. At this stage of study, psychological, social, and cultural factors appear to be more critical than physical factors.

6. In any case, persistent homosexual attraction demands the best pastoral and psychological care.
7. God in Christ loves, forgives, and accepts *all* people, also those with homosexual tendencies. Nothing is clearer in His revelation of Himself in the Scriptures.
8. God in Christ promises the power to heal disease, to overcome evil, to change patterns of living. His mercy makes us people of possibility. His mercy uses all the resources of His creation, such as medicine, psychiatry, psychology, counseling.
9. His Spirit helps us in our weakness (Romans 8).

WHAT TO DO

Many young people face masturbation and homosexuality as part of the power struggle. What to do about it:

Face the problem.

Tackle the cause as well as the symptom. More than occasional masturbation is a symptom. And has to be faced, of course. The cause is normally deeper and often more difficult to face. It may be lack of confidence, a feeling of rejection, or fear of failure, real or imagined.

Don't be afraid to admit where things have gone wrong. But at the same time, hang on to Him who makes things right, Jesus the Christ, tempted in every way as we are but victorious in the power struggle for us.

The most practical help is the most difficult: finding someone with whom to talk about the problem. God still works effectively through people. It's not always easy to find someone who knows how tough the power struggle is and who is willing to share in an open and trusting relationship. Sometimes it can be one of your parents. That's best when it works. Your pastor may fill the bill. Others have found a high school counselor helpful.

DOIN' WHAT COMES NATURALLY

(Or: Making Up Your Mind About Going All the Way!)

The title of this chapter indicates we ought to know one another well enough to level about what seems to really come on big in the lives of many young people: "going all the way,"[9] or sex before marriage.

Many books wade right into discussion of sexual humor, "sexy" clothes, dancing, necking, petting, etc., but skirt the intensity of the problem of high school premarital intercourse. Some counselors of youth believe that 30 to 40 percent of American young people have sexual intercourse outside of marriage during their high school years. In some circles it's called "going all the way" and includes mutual masturbation to orgasm. The church words for "going all the way" (intercourse outside of marriage) are "fornication" (every kind of unlawful sexual intercourse by an unmarried person) and "adultery" (voluntary sexual intercourse between a married person and someone who is not the lawful spouse). People inside and outside the church tend to use these two words interchangeably.

chapter

6

ME

A word of personal privilege before we start: There's a real danger in writing a book like this with the impression that my own "sexual path has been smooth," at least since those long-ago years of adolescence. This is not true. Teen-agers have no corner on the desire to make out. Most adults I know with any degree of intimacy, female and male, admit that sexual temptations did not disappear when the man in the collar pronounced them husband and wife.

The same is true for me.

In fact, at times I feel that people who work person-to-person

with people, including church professionals, are more con-
fronted by sex and sexual temptations than others. Maybe
it's caused by the intensity of working consciously with ideals.
Maybe it's caused by the demand for sensitivity and open-
ness to others, including their sexual needs. Undoubtedly
it's caused by no small crew of those "spiritual agents from
the very headquarters of evil" whom St. Paul talked about.

Let it be publicly known that temptation is real for all human
beings. And clergymen are human beings. It is real for me.
The opportunity to abuse sexuality can pop up in the weirdest
places—at a funeral or while preaching, distributing the
Sacrament, teaching a class, preparing a Bible study. You
name it; that's where it can happen.

My point is simply this: ideals and goals can coexist with
frustration, failure, and struggle. This is another reason for
all of us—youth and adults, youth and youth, adults and
adults—to be talking more deeply and more honestly about
life as it really is inside and around us.

50

End of word of personal privilege.

YOU

Now it's your turn. As you may guess, I didn't copy the above
paragraphs from a book. Nor did I write them so I could feel more
free to blast at you. I simply admitted I haven't "got it made" sexually
after 17 years of happy marriage (the adjective "happy" sounded corny
in that phrase, but it belongs there). And I believe you haven't got
everything neatly resolved either.

Not having all the answers, I realize, is small comfort and even
smaller help for leveling about "going all the way." One serious trouble
is that so many people pretend they have it all figured out. I doubt
that anyone will stop to check sexual pros and cons in the front seat
of a parked car. The heart often rules or overrules the head in sexual

decisions. But reasoned argument can come only from the deliberation of the head. And that decision has to be made beforehand. If the head is clear on the matter, there's perhaps less chance of its being over-ruled later by the heart.

So let's take a closer look at the increased popularity of "going all the way." The paragraphs that follow attempt to describe the reasons, known or unknown, spoken or unspoken, which underlie a more or less no-holds-barred approach to going all the way. Perhaps you've heard better reasons given. We'll stick to these five.

REASONS FOR "GOING ALL THE WAY":

Reason No. 1: The potentials of petroleum, prophylactic, and penicillin have radically changed the "conditions" for sexual behavior.

> The anonymity of the automobile (petroleum) whisks the young couple from concerned eyes and provides a heated parlor-bedroom wherever it's parked. Going all the way is easier.

> The availability of the pill (prophylactic) or other contraceptives dismisses the fear of pregnancy from most determined minds. Going all the way is safer.

> The antibodies of medical science (penicillin) promise that most forms of venereal disease can now receive adequate treatment. Although VD remains a serious and growing problem among teen-agers, going all the way is "cleaner" than ever before.

Reason No. 2: A certain amount of premarital sexual experimentation is more likely to lead to a happy marriage than to an ill-adjusted one — a most important consideration.

Mechanically, this view asserts that experience is the best teacher and that a period of apprenticeship or practical preparation has rarely harmed a vocation as serious as marriage.

Psychologically, this view holds that loving increases the capacity and the desire to love and therefore will normally contribute to a marriage rather than disturb it.

Reason No. 3: If (a) effective prevention against pregnancy is taken and if (b) two people have the kind of relationship which includes openness, genuine concern for the other, and if (c) they possibly have even promised to marry each other, premarital sex can be a meaningful and God-pleasing experience, "a real, mutual ministry."

Relationship is paramount. If the relationship is honest and helpful, the means for expressing it, such as mutually acceptable premarital intercourse, is not the primary concern. It's people who count.

Life is changing faster today. People seem helpless. No one cares; everyone fakes it out. In this kind of world a real relationship, even if it fights past morality, is worth developing to the fullest.

If premarital here refers to people who plan to marry someday, the only obstacles to going all the way are pertinent civic laws (if any) and the inconvenience of secrecy and deception until the wedding.

Reason No. 4: Morality is on the move; even the church is changing. Biblical answers not only sound outmoded, they *are* outmoded. They were designed for another people in another culture in another day.

> The church waited too long to say a positive word about sex. Rules and regulations alone have failed. Now it's too late. No one inside or outside the church cares what the church says anymore.

> In times of transition we just can't be sure of the answers. In fact, it may be that there are no answers, at least not more of the neatly boxed kind we've been used to.

Reason No. 5: Everyone's doing it.

> Well, at least a lot more than most people ever dream! It includes the "best" and the "worst" of the high school population. Many feel pretty guilty about it. Not many are stopping.

> Besides, some parents see to it that their high school daughters are on the pill, just in case. What's the sense of fighting it? The college crowd gave in years ago.

> And is it really any different from what's happening with adults? Really?

THANKS, BUT . . .

Please excuse me as I jump into "direct speech" to respond to the five reasons for "going all the way."

"First, thanks for being so frank. You probably haven't covered

53

all the reasons advanced someplace along the line. But what you've said, you've said pointedly. And at many points your words make sense.

"But the case you make doesn't hold together. You have quietly and effectively chosen those considerations that keep things going for 'doin' what comes naturally.'

"You assumed no concern from God, no hint at His interest, no awareness of His presence and power.

"You dodged or distorted the serious meanings of intercourse, sexuality, love, relationship.

"You want what you want when you want it. That's nice, but who's running the show? You? I doubt it. Me? I hope not. Who?

"Frankly, your personal happiness is not—repeat, not—the most important consideration in the world. There are other concerns and considerations. A part of maturity is to face them squarely.

"And to be sure, 'doing what comes naturally' won't work in all areas of life. Just try driving down the wrong side of the highway 'because I feel like it.' Or taking food or merchandise from a store without paying simply because you 'want' it.

"The word from God is that the love of God is the source of human love. In all its forms and expression it reflects and responds to His prior love for us. God's love forms and 'informs' our love."

Too much? How do we translate these nice words in terms of "going all the way"?

ANSWERS TO REASONS FOR "GOING ALL THE WAY"

ANSWER TO "Reason No. 1":

Fast-changing, industrial products like petroleum, prophylactic, and penicillin are a flimsy basis for personal decisions, especially ones which most people agree have deep emotional, social, and spiritual implications. Might as well consider burglary as a trade because better tools and faster getaway cars improve chances for not getting caught.

The issue is *not* "thou shalt not get caught" in one way or another. The real question is: What's the right way, and therefore the best way, before God and man, to use our gifts of sexuality for each other?

ANSWER TO "Reason No. 2":

This statement is a cross between a pure guess and a fond hope.

It begs the question whether premarital sexual experimentation is right or wrong. If it's okay to experiment, you still have to prove it's helpful toward a happy marriage. If it's wrong to experiment, you can't pin hopes for a happy marriage on it.

Inhibitions (whatever keeps you from "doin' what comes naturally") are not all bad. Yet many have simply grown out of traditions in society or out of distorted understanding of God's view and purpose of sexuality. Frequently inhibitions hinder a happy marriage.

But there's absolutely no guarantee that premarital sexual experimentation is helpful in overcoming inhibitions. In fact, clinical studies indicate that often the *least desirable* mechanical and psychological factors are at work in short-term "experimental" sexual relationships. "Statistically speaking (according to Kinsey), a majority of those whose marriages flounder have had pre-marital sexual experience." [10]

And besides, there are other live options for getting rid of harmful sexual inhibitions.

ANSWER TO "Reason No. 3":

This is the toughest argument so far. Relationship *is* paramount in all of life.

But that's not the only story nor the whole story. There are good and bad relationships. And no relationship exists by itself, in a vacuum. Because some people label premarital sexual experience in certain circumstances as "meaningful" or "helpful" does not make it right, God-pleasing, or a "ministry."

Take a good look at these considerations:

1. When things seem to be falling apart, it is all the more important to be particular about the nature and purpose of relationships. Is any relationship really better than none?

2. Ninety-nine percent of premarital sexual relationships isolate the pleasures and relations of sex

from the overall responsibility of personal relations between man and woman, "the awesome problem of creatively unifying two lives."

3. God's from-the-shoulder word is: Build solid heterosexual relationships, but save intercourse exclusively for the lifelong unifying relationship of marriage.

As for premarital relations by those pledged to become married, (a) watch out for attempting "to try out" one another like a new hat or new car, (b) don't forget the trial run is far different from the real-life, long-term course, and (c) observing legitimate civic laws is right, God-pleasing, and a "ministry."

ANSWER TO "Reason No. 4":

Sure the church is changing. It's made up of people like you, determined to grow in knowledge, wisdom, and spirituality. That's a mark of stability, not of weakness. Are you ready to serve as *the* judge as to which parts of our heritage are outmoded and which are not? How about lying, killing, and stealing? Are prohibitions against them outmoded? They're Biblical "answers." Or are you going to be selective? And if so, on what basis?

Admitting that people in all of history have been adept in shaping God and God's Word to fit their needs and times, how do we escape the same trap? How can we let God be God in the midst of our hypersensitive sexual age?

ANSWER TO "Reason No. 5":

This is by far the weakest argument. It ought to fall of its own sheer, dead weight.

The world is filled with all kinds of people. There's probably someone somewhere doing anything you or someone else wants to do. The whole college crowd didn't give in. And even if they did, what a primitive, crummy, and unhuman way to live: simply do what others do!

Besides, many of those "doing it" may well wish to God they could stop. — Let's face it, sexual fulfillment in terms of intercourse is not a gilt-edged promise or an irrevocable birthright at any age. Some people just haven't grown up enough to recognize this truth.

LAW AND LOVE

We have leaned over backward in these last paragraphs and imported extra quotation marks in an attempt to listen to "both sides" of the story. It's hard to judge if we've been fair. The dilemma now is to speak to these "reasons" while walking the tightrope between a rigid "all questions have been answered" and a flimsy "it's really up to you." Bible passages are easily gathered to support my point of view. But how does the Word from God get through to those in the middle of serious struggle?

The point is, there are few Christian youth who do not know exactly what the church says God's will is about premarital sexual activity. It's *not* a matter of telling them this. One thing the church has accomplished with the youth is to give them a fairly good idea of what the Ten Commandments are against. But I know many of these same youth aren't "impressed" with it at all.

This may well be youth's fault completely. But remembering a number of things our Lord said to religious leaders of His day, I am not willing to hang the entire rap on you. We adults, parents and church leaders, haven't come through as we want to or as we should.

And yet we have rights too: the right to be experienced, to be concerned, to be true to ourselves and to our convictions, along with the possibility of being wrong. I've no doubt about God's willingness to speak to men through men in His Word. My concern is with the decisions I have to make for Him, the understanding I have of His Word, the means I choose to share the faith and love He gives. No wonder God sends His Spirit "to straighten our words out" when we speak for and in Him.

> It takes *law* and *love*. God is "God-ly." He is on the one hand His holy, beyond-us-all self. His being and presence put us in our place as creatures who cannot be what He made us to be. His Word clues us that the wages of this, our sin, is death.

> And on the other hand, this same God is "man-ly," involved with the hairs of our head, the shirt on our back, the food on our table, and determined to give us Himself.

> His holiness makes clear who and what the standard is: God Himself. His love in Christ makes clear who makes living within that standard, living for God, with God, and in God possible.

> It's like believing in Christ.

> It *is* believing in Christ, our Savior and Lord.

In His Son, sexuality means to be liberated from social pressures and cultural conformity, to be free to say no as well as yes without feeling hopelessly square, and even to be able to live hopefully in the middle of sexual uncertainty.

it happens every day

IT HAPPENS EVERY DAY

Statistically speaking, marriage has never been so popular. More people marry, marry younger, and even the great majority of divorcees remarry. In spite of our more-or-less anti-institutional age, the institution of marriage is "in." It happens every day.

Although marriage may be some years away for you, it plays a significant role in your life right now. Puberty, sexual awareness, friendships, dating, education, selection of a vocation—all these are oriented toward marriage, even if you don't ever get married. In one way or another "marriage is a future which operates in the present for youth in very real ways."

Up to this chapter we've been talking about sex, sexuality, and love. This is appropriate because they come first. Marriage does not produce sexuality and love. Love and sexuality undergird marriage. As usual in Christian perspective, love comes first. Within this priority of love we live and move and "are for real," also in marriage.

And that's good.

But marriage is not a kind of magic wand, the waving of which makes everyone live happily ever after. The divorce rate alone should convince us of the tragic failures of personal relationships within marriage. That too happens every day. Marriage is called an institution, an effort to organize and regulate relationships. It isn't just the result of impulses. The divorce rate proves it has to be worked at.

In spite of all the more or less legitimate criticisms of the institution of marriage, Christian ethics insists that it is the proper place for love. *Marriage provides love its best opportunity to develop.* We say this neither to support traditional moral standards, which today are rapidly becoming obsolete, nor to attack the immorality and amorality of our time. We defend marriage not simply because it "offers the best fulfillment of the sex life" or because "parenthood brings to love a social dimension which demands continuity and stability." For the Christian, marriage is rooted in the manner in which God Himself loves us.[11]

Strangely enough, the Bible does not define marriage. It describes it and states its purpose. It doesn't say *how* two people become married. Leaving parents, establishing a permanent relationship, and becoming "one flesh" are the only things consistently mentioned in Genesis, in the Gospels, and by the apostles. Approval of parents and community is implied but not directly commanded. "Marriage is a lifelong union of a man and a woman unto one flesh. Scripture says no more than that regarding its essence."[12]

Marriage is the guardian of love, in imitation of the way in which God Himself loves. He provided man with symbols and reminders of His love and covenant: the rainbow, Sabbath, temple, miracles, sacraments, the record of His acts among men, especially the visit of His Son. So human love also has its symbols: promises spoken, wedding rings, signed documents, children. We need visible evidences. God's institution of marriage aids and supports love.

IT'S NOT EASY

Marriage is not easy. Hollywood, cozy honeymoon snapshots, and *Better Homes and Gardens* often try to make it look easy. Marriage is an arrangement for living together in love. But living together is complex. And although we don't know it at the time, the love we promise isn't the romantic version of soft music, moonlit nights, or automatic sexual pleasure. It's the love of hurried schedules, burnt toast, frazzled nerves, and unpaid bills—the love that covers a multitude of sins.

So marriage means maturity, and maturity, someone has said,

depends on the ability to combine satisfaction and frustration. It's the old "give and take" pattern. The relationship takes time, effort, sacrifice, patience, and endurance. It gives love, meaning, security, pleasure, and (often) wisdom. The ups and downs contribute to the meaning of the marriage. The growing satisfaction which husband and wife receive from their sexual life is in proportion to their growing devotion to each other.

All this emphasizes the seriousness of getting ready for marriage and why the Christian marriage ceremony stresses *faithfulness* (the pledge), *exclusiveness* (forsaking all others), and *permanence* (till we part in death). Christian marriage begins with you, the kind of person you have been, you are, and want to be. In order to love someone else, you have to be able to love yourself. In order to deny yourself, give yourself, sacrifice yourself, you have to have a "self" to deny or give or sacrifice. This is our call to be human.

God makes you possible as a human being. His "kingdom" is all the bother He went through to make you His person, fully human again. If He is for you, who can make it being against you? Your job is to accept the fact that you are accepted through the life, death, and resurrection of His Son. That's what Baptism is all about: direct, personal, lively involvement in the death and resurrection of Christ. The result of God's massive laundromat: you've never seen things so clean! Everything is fresh and new. The past is finished and gone. You are a completely new person.

ONE

The contrast between the faithfulness of God and the continued changing of man seems to be a hopeless contradiction. But the contradiction began to be resolved when the Son of God became incarnate, when Christ was born as a human being. Love was made flesh. Real love came down to our level and was made human. Of His own will God voluntarily limited, or "pulled in," His fantastic, indescribable love. He directed, controlled, and shaped it for the good of man. His boundless love is custom-made to fit our needs and abilities.

And this is a demonstration of what can happen to our human love, generally and especially within marriage. God tailored His love for man. Man's love in turn, our intense and growing love, need not be ashamed to humble itself and accept restraints, limitations, direction, and control. God shows us how love can abondon its claims to freedom and power and shape itself into faithfulness in marriage.

Freedom does not in fact have any value in itself. Its only meaning is in relation to love. The expression "free love" (meaning no restrictions on sexual intercourse) is not only false, it is a contradiction in terms. Any conflict between love—no matter how wholesome, "humble," or godly—and marriage arises from an unwillingness to accept the meaning of the Incarnation. In Christ, God has involved Himself with us in life and willingly accepts the limitations this demands. This kind of giving of Himself to us is both the source and the pattern of our giving ourselves to one another in marriage. His grace fulfills what we're unable to do. Faithfulness in marriage is godly, possible, and exciting. In Him it happens every day.[13]

ONLY

Marriage as a guardian of love is exclusive. Forsaking others, even father and mother, is not odd to Christian thought and life. God's people of old were shown the positive values of exclusiveness. It is not hostile, selfish, or evil. Its purpose is good, just as the exclusive hour of suffering and death for Christ was good. Only the healing of *His* exclusive presence, promise, and love makes "life together" possible. This is the power of Christ's resurrection made new in us. Every marriage is a miracle.

ALWAYS

"Sunday, Monday, or always?"

Songwriters make a mint, I suppose, out of our deep longing for "permanent" love. We want it to be the same always. But time gets in the way. Time changes things, makes things and persons old, and always brings the new. We are imprisoned by time.

And so is marriage. Things get changed and people get old. That which is new, less scarred by time looks better. Time gets in the way.

Again God's love overcomes. His love broke into time and remade it into the servant of man. Time is no longer the enemy of love. Our days are given us in Christ to spend in loving. To speak of time therefore is to speak of love. We love within time, against time, and with time. We know that with each moment our loved one will be changed just as time changes us. But our time is in His hand. His grace in Christ makes it clear that time was made for man, not man for time. "Till we part in death" is a promise of love and a statement of faith.

MIRACLE-MYSTERY

The road to marriage is the route to mystery. Love and sexuality have been advertised, biologized, psychologized, romanticized, sociologized until there's almost nothing left. People still buy "true confession" magazines in a weird desire to see more behind the scenes of "love." We seem to want everything exposed or explained.

Yet marriage is a mystery as well as a miracle.

No one can draw a picture or make a chart to show you what happens to a husband and wife. Until you are married, you have to take the word of those who are. That's the limitation of all study of sexuality. What really counts can't be seen.

It's a mystery.

It is the mystery of being known. The Hebrews used the verb "to know" to describe the sexual experience of husband and wife. For them "knowing" meant more than intellectual recognition of a person. It meant involvement and participation with that person in experiences designed to reveal his true identity.

Husband and wife "become one flesh." That doesn't mean simply that they have intercourse. That means they are really so close to each other—mentally, emotionally and physically—that they consider themselves as being one. To become one flesh in marriage means each person abandons himself to the other. They communicate with each other in ways past describing. And the joy of knowing another person so fully develops continuously. Through this oneness each gets to know more about his own self. Together they find new meaning for life and new possibilities to love as each has been loved.

It's a mystery. It doesn't happen perfectly. Or all at once. Marriage grows on you. And it's great.

COMMUNICATION—COITUS

Sexual communication includes a whole range of experiences— from affectionate looks or tone of voice, playful banter, graciousness of manner and exchange of compliments, through hand-holding, hugging, kissing, necking, and petting to genital play and sexual intercourse. Relative satisfaction at any one step of this "ladder of desire" intensifies desire and creates a sense of urgency in seeking more intimacy—the next step.

> Coitus is God's special gift of communication to a married couple. It is the top step of the ladder, full sexual union, in which the penis of the husband penetrates the vagina of the wife with the emission of seminal fluid.

> In preparation for coitus, sexual communication causes excitement (erection) of the genitals of both wife and husband. All that takes place between them through sight, touch, talk, and smell belongs to and is part of this experience of sexual intercourse. The act is inherently vigorous, consuming a great deal of energy.

> The intense pleasure which is the climax of this experience is called orgasm. For the husband this accompanies the seminal emission through the penis. For the wife, orgasm is more complex, longer lasting, and experienced in the clitoris and, at a deeper level, in the vagina.

BABIES

Marriage does not achieve its complete fulfillment within itself. Other than for exceptional reasons, there is no true married love without the wish to have children. Wife and husband are physically and psychologically designed and equipped for parenthood. The whole biological process is focused on the bearing of children.

> Parenthood makes love actual by giving it visible continuity. We celebrate birthdays as "religious" events, for children are evidence of the mercy of God. "Every child that comes into the world brings the message that God has not yet despaired of man."[14]

> A child is not a cure-all and in fact can become the object of conflict between parents. But "two beings are never more truly one than when they become three" — another dimension of the mystery and miracle of sexuality and marriage.

EN ROUTE

Babies may be way off in your future. But parenthood grows out of marriage, which grows out of courtship and love, which usually grow out of dating. So you're en route, even if you're only at the "wanting a date" stage.

Dating usually starts with attraction to some members of the opposite sex. We want to be with them, talk with them, listen to them, and get to know them as persons.

Naturally the body is involved since we are whole persons and react with our whole beings. So there is desire for physical contact as well. A boy wants to touch. A girl wants to be touched. The touch is pleasant. The touch is power. It can be casual and restrained. It can arouse more sexual desire than either girl or fellow is equipped to handle.

> Three things to remember: (a) physical contacts are related to mental and emotional processes; (b) a boy is usually more conscious of his sexual nature and physical sensations of sex than a girl; (c) a boy is easily aroused sexually.

If we want to control and direct the power of sex, we have to impose limits on the pleasure of sex. And limits on pleasure are never popular. Like it or not, life has its limits. To accept this reality is a mark of maturity.

The purpose of dating and courtship is to give the relationship between a girl and a fellow the opportunity to test out what they may have in common. A balance between sex and other interests is obviously necessary for a constructive relationship. As people impose limits on sex while they are getting to know each other, they move into the position of looking for and cultivating other interests.

Sex in human beings is complex. We have seen that it cannot be separated from the rest of life. The amount of time spent together during dating and courtship is more significant than whether or not you consider yourselves to be going steady. Human motives, our own as well as those of others, are tough to figure out. In dating and courtship you have the chance to recognize attitudes and actions that take advantage of others. Behavior that exploits others defeats relationship and love.

But getting ready for marriage is fun. Dating, getting around, and getting acquainted is meant to be a ball. There are loads of different and interesting people in the world. Openness and patience can lead to the one with whom you can enjoy the faithfulness, exclusiveness, and permanence of marriage. It's great, and it happens every day.

P. S. Marriage must be approached with eyes wide open. Be sure to look at the consistent warning that interfaith (between Christians of different denominations) and interracial marriages are difficult and often inadvisable. But they are not wrong or forbidden. Keep your eyes wide open.

P. P. S. We must also be alert for any subtle insinuation that those who do not get married are inferior in any way. There are dangers in marriage and dangers in singleness. In either, God's will can be achieved in love. The church can assist by discovering valid ways to help single people enjoy their sense of sexuality in an impersonal society where marriage at times seems to be the only acceptable pattern of life.

as you travel

AS YOU TRAVEL

In one way, when it comes to recognizing, understanding, and "living with" your sexuality, you're on your own.

It's terribly personal, as we've seen.

It's powerful.

It can't be operated with a checklist of do's and don'ts.

So in one way of thinking, you are on your own.

But that's not the only way of thinking about it, and from my point of view it's not the best way of thinking about it. For we're in this together. The whole human race turns out to be sexual. And that means that all of us, at different stages, are in the struggle of recognizing, understanding, and living with sexuality as a gift and opportunity from God.

chapter

8

Besides, one of the incomparable values of Christianity is that we're *never* on our own — in time of struggle or of success. The promise of our Lord is clear about that. That's probably why so many young people I know say that one of their favorite passages of Scripture is: "I am with you always, even to the end of the world." (Matthew 28:20)

The God who sometimes seems "afar off," often when we seem to want and need Him most, is really a God at hand, even when we don't know or recognize or admit it. And to top it off, He "who fills heaven and earth" also provides people to "be with us" in the struggle. More than a few are around at different times with varying kinds of helpfulness. Why not, "as you travel, ask them"?

You may want to use the following as your own confidential checklist of personal resources for the sexual highways and byways:

Person (Add others of your choice)	Qualifications (You know them better than I do!)	Availability (Getting to them when you need them)	Helpfulness (Meeting you where you are)
MOTHER	_____	_____	_____
FATHER	_____	_____	_____
PASTOR	_____	_____	_____
TEACHER	_____	_____	_____
RELATIVE	_____	_____	_____
FRIEND (adult)	_____	_____	_____
FRIEND (your age)	_____	_____	_____
SCHOOL COUNSELOR	_____	_____	_____
PHYSICIAN (family doctor)	_____	_____	_____
OTHERS	_____	_____	_____
	_____	_____	_____
	_____	_____	_____

It's really not very sharp to attempt to evaluate people in this way. The evaluation, if accurate at all, will probably change before the week or month or year is out. The real point is to show there are people around who are really "designed" to be with you in your development as a sexual person.

DECISIONS

As we travel, we make decisions about sexual relationships every day. How do we know we're right? Or, at least, how do we get to feel right about our decisions?

At least four approaches to determining our sexual behavior are currently popular:

1. Try not to pay any attention to the struggle. Because it's so difficult, play it by ear. Relax and try to be natural.
2. Get a good set of rules to cover everything, or almost everything, and live with them. It's safest this way.
3. "Love" is the *one* deciding factor. If "love" is supreme, do whatever you think grows out of or leads to "love."
4. A combination of 2 and 3 — love for fellow human beings plus a set of moral rules which provide the best of our knowledge, thought, and experience.

No. 1 is an impossible attempt to escape responsibility. No. 2 minimizes man's integrity as a human being capable of decision. No. 3 sounds best but is the most tricky and is terribly difficult. It is equally impossible because love is *not* the only valid motive in the world. Besides, it's impossible to evaluate our own motives in emotion-filled moments. No. 4 is not simple or easy either, but of the current options it offers the most. It is honest and realistic. It makes our motives the primary consideration but gives significant weight to rules which are for all practical purposes universally valid.

DATING

Dating is a very important means for learning about control of sexual power. Let's test approach No. 4 on several of the most-asked questions about dating:

What does it take to get dates? ". . . the same thing it takes to get and be a friend."

"You must have some likeable qualities. (Everyone does, but there is always room for improvement.) Besides this, you must have the ability to appreciate and like others. . . .

"If you want dates, look for them among those with whom you have something in common. . . . This common interest gives you something to talk about." [15]

What do you do on a date? That depends on a great many things: ". . . who you are, where you live, what the possibilities are, whom you are going with, what you can do, what you like to do, how much money you have to spend, what your parents consider permissible, and above all, the ingenuity and imagination you possess for inventing ways of having a good time." [16]

The most important thing is to get to know each other. This can happen on a group date as well as singly. It can happen on a walk, at a football game, while bowling, after a movie, at a party. Sometimes it's all fun—kidding, laughing, joking. Sometimes it's dead serious. Be ready for both. And be willing to talk—about anything from outer space to inner beliefs. Youth is a time for learning about people. Dating is a way to do it.

How about kissing, necking, and petting? Physical contact is an important means of communication. It's almost impossible to date without physical contact. It's the range and meaning of the contact that counts. And that depends on you, your maturity of feeling, and your control of your sex impulses.

74

"Control of sex is not a matter of putting on the brakes. It is not merely a matter of don't do this and don't do that. Control means directing, guiding, and restraining your sexual impulses for a purpose." [17]

The straight word is: some restricted physical contact on a date is inevitable and normally desirable. This includes kissing. Your view of yourself and your partner dictates where you stop. "The only good honest reason for petting is as a limited expression of warm liking or real love." [18]

Necking and petting are tricky and dangerous. It's easy to offend yourself, your partner, and God, who reserves the fullest enjoyment of the body for marriage. The only guaranteed 100-percent-or-your-money-back safeguard is "Don't pet at all."

But almost everybody does. . . .

"The way to enjoy it with safety is for each boy and girl to decide for himself, while he is alone, able to think undisturbed by any sexual stirrings, and without application to any one person or situation, how far he wants to go, and how to distinguish the yellow and red lights that signal when, where and how to stop." [19]

What's going too far? Anything against the will of God or your conscience is "too far." Usually the meaning of the expression ranges from fondling a girl's covered or uncovered breasts, to caressing the lower portions of the body from the thighs to the vulva, to noncoital orgasm (sexual climax without insertion of the penis), to intercourse.

Girls are often pressured into sexual experimentation by the dare to "prove your love."

Ann Landers lays it on the line about going too far: "Usually the girl persuades herself that the boy cares a great deal for her, so what she is doing really isn't wrong after all. . . . Call it 'narrow-minded,' 'mid-Victorian,' 'puritanical' or whatever may come to mind, but sex outside of marriage is unacceptable in our society. This conflict can play havoc with the nervous system — and often does." [20]

For the Christian "too far" *is* too far because of relationships. Our guide is the relationship we have to each other through the relationship we have to God in Christ. Our control is set for the purpose of letting every expression of our sexuality reflect His will, His love, *and* His limits.

What about going steady? There are all kinds of going steady. One girl said she went steady for one hour in her junior year at high school. The other end of the spectrum is the "You belong to me and I belong to you" type. These couples see each other every hour at school, having a standing date for each weekend and following a strict hands-off policy with other fellows and girls.

This kind of going steady cheats you of the opportunity to learn about all kinds of people. "Dating years are precious. They are years during which you develop patterns and techniques for dealing with people. A free-wheeling dating arrangement will give you confidence and teach you social skills. The challenge of adjusting to new situations will keep you alert. The ability to get along with all types of personalities – even the wacky ones – will be a valuable asset through-out your life." [21]

Can you tell when you are really in love? There are all sorts of feelings for all sorts of persons, and we have no "love-meters" as yet. The well-known writer about love and the facts of life, Evelyn Millis Duvall, suggests the following six "tests" for evaluating real love:

> Love is outgoing
> Real love relaxes energy
> Love wants to share
> Love is a we-feeling
> You must like as well as love
> Time is the surest test[22]

Is your love like this? Only you can really tell.

When shall I marry? "The time for marrying comes when there is a combination of four conditions:
> When there is the degree of maturity that marriage demands
> When marrying will be in harmony with other goals
> When circumstances are favorable, i. e., sufficient income, your own living quarters, approval of both families
> When you have found, and love, the right person
If all these conditions are satisfied, you can marry with confidence. If one of them is lacking, you take an unnecessary risk.
> Of the four, the most important is maturity. . . ." [23]

The ability you develop in answering questions for yourself about dating or any other sexual relationship hinges on your understanding of sexuality as a means God has given you for expressing yourself. Books can only help you think things through for yourself. If you're hung up on specific questions, the following paperbacks are among the best listed in the "Books" section on pages 107 – 108: *Love, Sex and Life* by Marjory Bracher, *Love and the Facts of Life* by Evelyn Millis Duvall, *Youth Considers Sex* by William E. Hulme, *Sex and the Adolescent* by Maxine Davis, and *Ann Landers Talks to Teen-Agers about Sex* by Ann Landers.

Lest we forget: These books stand in relation to God's Book. Its message about His Son informs our decisions on dating, marriage, and all of life. In fact the decisions we make as we travel are fashioned in continuing conversation with the Word and the world to which He calls us. And it's a conversation in which all Christians are joined. Which takes us back to the opening paragraphs of this chapter: we're not really on our own. Christians are related to each other. We carry one another's burdens, share each other's joys. We speak the Word to each other and to the world we love.

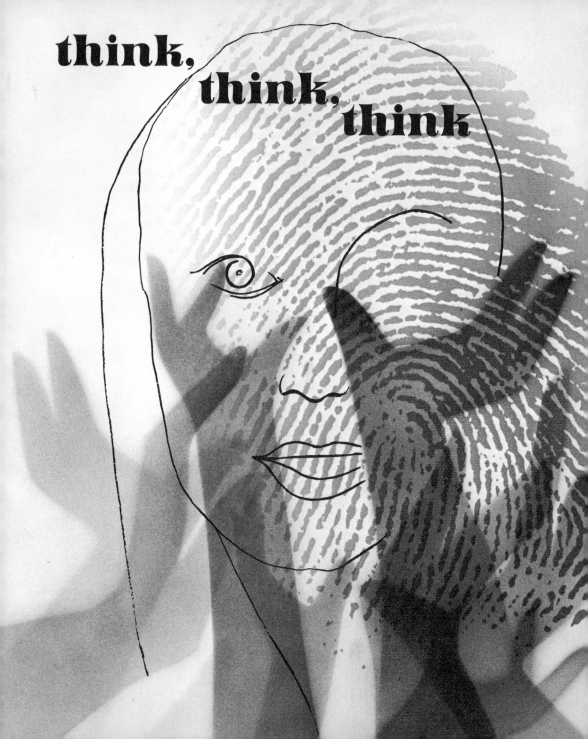

think, think, think

THINK, THINK, THINK

Just to prove I haven't lost my touch as a bona fide representative of the adult generation, this chapter comes to you as a *pop quiz* on what we've been trying to talk about so far. It'll probably be no more helpful or effective than some of the ones in Biology 2, but it may help underline a serious matter I have in mind.

The point is that all of us rather consistently are bumping up against ideas and opinions of life and love and sexuality totally different from the one we've been working with. Sometimes we meet these point-blank in a friend or in print. Most of the time they're neatly packaged so we hardly know what's hit us. The question is: How well can you spot the "distinctions"? How would you fare in testing the ideas of others against where you are now in your thinking about sexuality?

chapter

9

The pop quiz is divided into six sections of varying difficulties and length. Answer the questions for each; mark your own paper, if you like. Or just for fun, ask someone else to take the quiz too and launch a full-fledged discussion.

Section One — **OPINION POLL**

In the spirit of our national opinion polls and magazine questionnaires, try the following true-false statements on for size (honor system, please):

1. Sexual intercourse is the best and deepest way to show love for another person.
2. A person who has not had sexual intercourse is a "virgin."
3. Knowledge about sex makes a person sexually adequate.
4. Premarital sex makes for a better married sex life.
5. Premarital sex ruins a good sex life in marriage.
6. Holding back sexually can create mental disorder.

7. Most married men had premarital experiences and are glad they did.
8. Sexual restrictions that haven't worked are wrong.
9. Love is the only honest basis for sexual intercourse.
10. Love is mostly feeling right about a person.

Can you explain why you answered the way you did? Which statement bothered you most? Which was most unfair? Which most obvious?

Section Two — A SHORT STORY

THE CONVENTION

The girl came through the door of Convention Hall and tilted her head in the direction of the huge sign that dominated the stage. "That Men May Know Christ!" it read.

She stopped and waited for the fellows to gather. It was always so wherever she went. Some stood awkward, back one pace. Others crowded and bantered. In general she enjoyed the banter more. After all it was the only life she knew. . . .

"Wow!" The word came almost spontaneously. "A dark-haired Marilyn Monroe," Barry muttered to himself. The girl wandered by like a presence. You felt her entrance without looking.

The conference was 10 minutes from beginning.

On the platform the treasurer of the conference saw her from a distance as he tried out his platform chair for size. An indistinct murmur escaped his lips.

"D'ya see what I see?" he said finally.

The president had a moment of superiority. "She came in our car."

"No kidding?" he asked as casually as possible.

"No kidding at all. Fact is, it's funny. She's not even very well liked at home."

"By the girls, I suppose. That's understandable."

"It's funny. Even the fellows are wary of dating her, I heard. She's not from my home town."

"She fast?"

"What do you think?"

"Well, my thoughts aren't very spiritual."

The treasurer exchanged a mutual trust glance with Ham Parker, the president . . . completing his last year in office. Barry moved with a certain assurance. He was Ham Parker's candidate for president. . . .

. . . .

One of the Eagle Run leaguers was sitting with the girl. With the service in progress, the boy had noticed her surface friendliness retreating to some incandescence, baffling and almost fearful to behold. An indescribable separation had been effected. The boy had already begun looking for another girl by the close of the keynote speech. He had found out one fact about her. Her nickname was Candy. . . .

At the Anchor Room Ham was telling the Bible study leader, "I know we promised to mention that everyone bring Bibles. We just forgot. I somehow thought you were giving a speech."

After a continuing skirmish, Ham compromised, "Look, maybe we can get the passage typed up and run off on mimeograph tonight. Barry probably could do it if he can get someone to type. I hope you realize that means he'll miss the skating party."

"A friend is a friend," Barry said to himself as he struck one-fingered at the hotel typewriter.

"Matthew 25:31-46. Gosh, I'll never get through it." He decided to take a break in the hotel lobby. Almost immediately he was aware that Candy was someplace. Her eyes caught his and he felt almost a reprimand. A tinge of guilt prompted him to nod and then go to her.

"Now this is a crime. They're going to give a prize to the most beautiful skater at the party and you're not there. Why," he sputtered in his own self-revelation, "you'd win in a walk!"

She flushed and then smiled, "Ham said you needed a typist. I can type."

"You can?"

"I had a B plus last year. My first year. I can do almost 45 words a minute."

"Boy, am I ever glad to hear that."

Then he was afraid again. And she.

She typed the passage, and then the pause became an eternity.

"Go to the skating party with me?" he almost asked. But was she Ham's girl? He'd play it safe.

"Tell you what. I owe you at least a Coke or something in the Coffee Shop. How about it?"

They sat talking. She was suddenly talking in torrents, as if she waited all her life to say something. She talked about herself. What it was to be lonely—to be beautiful. To her they were synonymous. How she knew she was sexy-looking. Her mother had told her many times. It almost seemed like. . . .

Barry listened perplexed. At one moment he wanted to cover her face with kisses; at another he found himself at the edge of panic.

Too beautiful, too beautiful for me, he was thinking. Suddenly Ham and the treasurer swept into the Coffee Shop. "Where have you been? We've been looking for you everywhere. I wanted you to give out the prizes. Man, if you want me to get you elected. . . ."

For a second Ham drew back, "Oh, oh! I see. Candy, tsk. No wonder, Barry! Candy, baby, tell him the convention is waiting."

Barry was stammering.

"You're here for a convention," Ham was saying. "What's a con-   82
vention for if you don't go to sessions?"

As they left Barry wasn't sure Candy could hear Ham speaking, "Man alive! Don't you know she's got sex written all over her? She's dynamite. There's not a guy from her town that would take her. Her pastor called *me* and asked if I had room!"

Barry tried to look back. He ran to get the mimeographed material, stopped at the Coffee Shop when he returned, but she was gone.

. . . .

At the morning breakfast, Barry and Ham heard a group of girls talking. "She was just awful. Her counselor couldn't do anything with her. And you know, she was asleep the night before when we came in. We talked till 3:00 a. m. and you know, she actually moaned as she slept. No wonder. With that kind of attitude!"

The words got lost for Barry, then the thread came through again.

"All day she literally screamed at everybody. They sent her home at noon. I've never seen anything like it."

"And so beautiful."

"Sexy is the correct word, girl."

"No wonder they call her Candy. Wonder what her real name is?"

Ham was saying, "Now there are some things you ought to be thinking about, Barry. This convention has gone all right, but there are a couple of mistakes we made. . . .

He saw that Barry wasn't hearing as they walked to the hall.

The Bible study leader was beginning, "Under the theme 'That Men May Know Christ,' let's read Matthew 25:31-46 together."

"When the Son of Man shall come in his glory and all his holy angels with him . . . ."

Ham whispered, "That Candy's a pretty lousy typist. Say, did you hear about her . . . ."

Barry nodded rapidly and read with the group, "And when did we see thee hungry and feed thee, or thirsty and gave thee drink? And when did we see thee . . . ."[24]

Questions about "The Convention":

1. **Why would the beautiful girl of the story have problems? Why might she be lonely even with many boys around her? Why would some boys be afraid of her?**
2. **What would the theme of the convention have to do with the central events that were occurring?**
3. **Would you want persons of the opposite sex to think of you as sexless, at least at times? Why?**
4. **If you had the opportunity and the courage, how would you have showed the girl that you cared about her as a person? How would you have tried to help the fellows see her as a person?**

SECTION THREE — AFFIRMATION

It's said that many Christians are more likely to feel guilty about sex than not. How do you react to this paraphrasing of the old-style "confession of sins" from the traditional Sunday worship service to an "affirmation of life"?

O almighty God, merciful Father, I, a rich, joyful saint by Thy fatherly mercy, profess unto Thee all my love and devotion with which I am ready to serve Thee, and willingly accept the hope of temporal and eternal life in Thee. But I am heartily in need of Thee and sincerely seek after Thee, and I pray Thee of Thy boundless mercy and for the sake of the holy, innocent, willing suffering and death of Thy beloved Son, Jesus Christ, to fill me with Thy Spirit that I may continue to serve Thee and all men as Thy rich and joyful servant!

Questions about the "affirmation of life":
1. **Do young people need to be told more about sin or more about forgiveness? Why?**
2. **Is the same true for adults? Why?**
3. **What keeps *you* humble in your life as a sexual person?**
4. **What makes you feel more confident as a sexual person?**

SECTION FOUR — **THE LORD BLESS YOU ... OUT THERE**

In the first century Christianity was called "the Way." This referred to Christ as "the Way" as well as to "the way" people lived. Another quite specific advantage for sexual Christians traveling "the Way" is their group worship. The denominations that have chosen to follow the traditions of the early church have special responsibilities to relate the "common worship experience" to the "particularities" of the individual worshipers.

I believe this "common service" lends itself to many aspects of our discussion of living an exciting, godly sexual life. It's not easy and often not very exciting. But then it's been said that group worship may well be the toughest work we do all week.

Here are some examples from the traditional Sunday morning worship service:

The Service	**On the Sexual Way**
THE CONFESSION OF SINS	Not only the abuse but our failure to use the blessed gift of our sexuality for God and others

THE ABSOLUTION	A solid reminder that God for Christ's sake accepts us by grace with our body, mind, and spirit
THE SCRIPTURE LESSONS (Old Testament, Epistle, Gospel)	God in the flesh dealing in judgment and mercy with man in the flesh
THE CREED	We affirm the presence of the Father, who conceived sexuality, the Son, who redeemed it, the Spirit, who chooses to make our sexual being His home (temple of the Holy Spirit)
THE OFFERTORY	The call for a clean heart, a right spirit, and the joy of salvation as we travel with the Holy Spirit
THE OFFERINGS	At the moment of "offering" to God our quarters, dimes, and dollars, we give Him also "our bodies as a living sacrifice" (see Romans 12:1-2)
THE LORD'S PRAYER	Literally loaded; for example: God's will to be done through our sexuality, the daily bread which supports our sexual body, deliverance from the temptations and evil which plague our sexual being
THE LORD'S SUPPER	The dramatic sharing of Christ's own body and blood along with bread and wine for sexual Christian beings to eat and drink, cele-

brating His death and resurrection, entering into deep and daily fellowship with Him and all Christians, receiving power for practical, sexual living

THE BENEDICTION

According to some, this blessing-prayer was meant not so much for the closing moment of common worship as for the opening moment of common life "back out in the world."

Understood in this sense, the Benediction becomes a powerful resource and reminder for sexual living: the Lord bless and keep you on that exciting, tricky, servantlike, fun-filled sexual life back in the world for which He made you, to which He called you, and into which He goes with you.

86

Questions about "The Lord Bless You ... Out There":
1. Have you ever thought of public worship as "sexual"?
2. Do you feel closer to God when you worship in church? Closer to people? Is this related to your sexuality? Why?
3. Where do you think the main thrust of Christian worship in your parish should be: repairing what's past? living today? preparing for heaven?
4. What do you think can be done to make worship come alive for youth? Will this help their understanding of sexuality? Why?

SECTION FIVE – **SEXUALITY ANONYMOUS**
This part of the quiz is for real because the excerpt that follows is from an unsolicited letter. It was written by a young Christian at-

tending college who learned that I was writing a book about sexuality and wanted to be sure I would honestly tell the full story of how "some" young people think today.

SEXUALITY ANONYMOUS
—an unsolicited description of the "new morality" by a young, serious-minded college student

If I rip behind the legalism of rules that try only to govern external behavior, i. e., no sexual intercourse prior to or outside of marriage, I come up with three presuppositions on which my "old morality" was based:

1. Sexual intercourse has the primary (if not only) purpose of childbearing.
2. Sexual intercourse is the highest form of expression of love between two people and should be used to express this ultimate love only.
3. This highest form of expression must be shared with only one person to be meaningful and must be shared within a structure of total commitment to that person, i. e., marriage.

If these three tenets are true, then I can see no alternative but to obey the rules my mother has recited to me.

I can only briefly suggest some of the issues involved in my suspicion that these are not true:

1. Issues involved: 20th-century population explosion, development of effective contraception, the physiological, psychological, and spiritual need for intercourse whether a couple intends to have children or not.
2. This is tricky. I guess one of the basic issues is the scepticism we have of any person eliciting "ultimate love" from us. Especially the scepticism that at the age of 21 or 22 we will choose a partner who will elicit a greater degree of love from us than any person we will meet in the future. Further, there

is the counterassumption that sexual intercourse need not be saved to express "ultimate love" but rather can express a great degree of love and concern without losing its significance or "using" another person.

3. This is trickier. Again, a scepticism that love is or should be this exclusive. Also, the experience that loving increases the capacity and the desire to love and hence causes one to deepen present relationships and seek out new ones.

Now I hope I haven't just set up a straw man and knocked it down. In any case, the end result, my "new morality" is currently made up of these guideposts:

Premarital sex involves at least two considerations: the possibility for children and the depth of feeling between the two people involved. If effective contraception is used and if two people have the kind of relationship which includes openness, genuine concern for the other, etc., etc., premarital sex can be a meaningful and God-pleasing experience—a real mutual ministry.

Questions about "Sexuality Anonymous":
1. **In which points do you agree with the writer? Why?**
2. **With what do you disagree? Why?**
3. **Do you think many young Christians may agree with the point of view presented in this quote?**
4. **Are there parts in this quote which could be *either* true or false? Which? Why do you think so?**
5. **If you disagree with this point of view, how would you attempt to answer this (obviously) talented person?**

SECTION SIX—1 **CORINTHIANS 13 REVISITED**

Although not everyone does or should like "paraphrases" of God's Word, here is one that turns out to be more of a sermon on the deeper understanding of our sexuality. It's most of chapter 13 of

1 Corinthians reverently restyled for this particular purpose:

Though I have all the physical assets of a playboy bunny
but have no love,
I become no more than flowering grass
or a sexual symbol.
If I have the gift of warmth and responsiveness
and know how to use it,
and if I have the power to make others respond to me,
but have no love,
I amount to nothing at all.
If I am willing to give my body to another,
with no strings attached,
but have no love,
I achieve precisely nothing. . . .

For if there are desires,
they will be fulfilled and done with.
If there are new moralities,
the need for them will disappear.
If there is "reality" of the moment,
it will be swallowed up in truth.
For our "reality" is always incomplete,
and our desire is always incomplete,
and when the complete comes,
that is the end of the incomplete. . . .

At present we are looking at sexuality
as at puzzling reflections in a mirror.
The time will come when we shall see reality
whole and face to face.
At present all I know is a little fraction of the truth,
but the time will come
when I shall know it as fully as God knows me!

Questions about "1 Corinthians 13 Revisited":
1. Is sexuality a "reality" to you now? If not, why not? If so, in what ways?
2. Is the love St. Paul wrote about "something added on top" of other virtues, or "something within" them all? Why?
3. Is it all right to love your sexuality? Why?

LIFE CAN BE SEXUAL . . . *NOW*

The nice thing about sexuality is that it's for right now!

The sad thing is that so many people think only in terms of sex (36-24-36, remember?) or sexiness. That's for right now too but usually turns out to be an overestimated flash-in-the-pan.

The best thing about sexuality is that it's for right now—and for the future. For sexuality is an important part of all our relationships. In a real way it's a medium of exchange between persons. It is the dynamic force (power, again!) that enables a human being to attain the goal of existing for others.

Sexuality is not only recognizing that you are female or male; it's what you understand femaleness and maleness to mean—and what you do with your femaleness and maleness as you serve others. It's love in depth, with your whole being.

> In this sense we can accurately say that our sexuality does not belong to us at all. It belongs to that other person—boy or girl, parent or friend, relative or neighbor, acquaintance or stranger—in and through whom it comes alive and develops, for the moment or for life.

PARENTS AND ALL THAT

Sexuality is for now, and it started with your parents. No denying that, no matter what their popularity status is with you at the moment. You undoubtedly recognize that we're not merely talking about the biological process through which you made your "grand entrance." Rather we mean that "young people's relationships with their contemporaries of both sexes are deeply colored by their fundamental relationships with fathers and mothers."

Parents happen to be one of the many forces that have been "working on" you and your sexuality for some time. Others have been in the act: grandparents, nice aunts and uncles, not-so-nice aunts and uncles, neighbors good and bad, your pastor, your kindergarten, elementary and high school teachers, including that good-looking one in study hall, not to forget, of course, your very own contemporaries.

So have the mass media—radio disc jockey, TV, magazines, movies, advertisers, etc.—been "working on" you. We're only beginning to understand their impact on us all. But we already have the facts about how crucial your relationship with your parents is. If you have the blessing of their still being "alive and kicking," life can be sexual with them . . . now.

For one thing, parents have needs too, you know—ones you may often be able to help with. They need to feel accepted and loved just as they are. Most of them need some kind of regularity or structure in their lives. And no matter how "ancient" you may think they are, parents also need freedom to grow as persons.[25]

Your sexuality has to express itself in love that has the power to "save." It may not look or sound or feel different, but this kind of love comes from the depth of our inside concern for others, from love that has been turned on by God Himself. And this means the acid test: to love when the person in need of our love is unlovable, not only in the sense of unattractiveness but in the sense of real personal antagonism. This includes people who hurt us, harm us, bug us, people who act or live in ways we don't understand or like, people who are radically different from us in attitude, temperament, faith, goals, or race. This is *crucial* ground for putting your whole sexual being to work . . . now.

94

"For if you love only those who love you"—guess who's being quoted!—"what credit is that to you?" Even young hoods do that! And if you exchange greetings only with your own clique, are you doing anything exceptional? Even the pagans do that much.

"But I tell you, love your enemies, and pray for those who persecute you, so that you may be sons of your heavenly Father."

Check it out for yourself, the fifth chapter of Matthew, Phillips' translation, slightly adapted.

DIALOG

You might as well get in on another fad if you haven't done so already. Everyone's been talking about, planning or preparing, going to or coming from some kind of "dialog." Dialog means a two-way communication between persons in which there is understanding, a real "flow of meaning" back and forth in spite of all the obstacles that normally would block the relationship.

Your sexuality helps dialog. Your opportunity *now* is to help let dialog happen, with those you know and those you don't know, with those you like and especially those you don't like. It's possible and it's urgent. How does it happen?

It starts with the other person—just seeing someone else as a person rather than as a 36-24-36 or a thing to be used or a means to some end you want or need, like an *A* in English, for instance. We must fight the mass-produced image of sex so it doesn't determine our understanding of sexuality. In reality, persons as they come, people you know right now, are the starting point for the dialog on sexuality.

95

Openness to persons as they are is the next step. This is not easy because it ordinarily demands that you be pretty sure of yourself first. And we often aren't sure of ourselves. Which is the very reason we've been pounding away at the big word from God: that He accepts and loves us as we are . . . sent His Son as evidence of this love . . . affirmed it in a big way on the big day of His resurrection. God is for us so we can be for others.

Consciously moving into full-blown, open relationship with others, female or male, on their terms, is exciting. It is the opportunity to create the desire for that person to grow to his or her greatest potential. This comes through an atmosphere of trust so the person need not be fearful or defensive but can freely face the challenge of the relationship. This breeds the excitement of *wanting* to develop all our potential. You can't beat it.

This is not the same as nagging or needling a person or giving the I'd-like-to-do-a-complete-repair-job-on-you impression. It's the process of "losing yourself," body, mind, spirit, and all, in the involvement with others. The truth is, in that process you find your own sexual personality developing.

And you get to know the joy of being a person to whom other people respond; you get a feeling of power in the best and most helpful sense because things have happened through the being that is you.

That's godly joy. It's Christlike living.

Dialog, or openness to meet and help people as they are, is risky business. Someone can get hurt and often does. Our Lord did. We are called to be like Him: willing to take the risk because the Father asks us. That's part of seeking first His kingdom and righteousness. He guarantees to take care of the rest.

DISCIPLINE

Living sexually now in dialog with others who need our love demands discipline. Doing only what comes naturally doesn't fill the bill, we said. Love for others needs to be controlled, directed, shaped to the opportunities and limitations of people, faith, and the moment.

Discipline is the self-control we exercise over ourselves and our relationships with others. Take necking and petting, for instance. The question, "How far can I go?" really isn't the right question. The right question is: "What am I doing to and with a person of worth, right now?" and: "How does what I'm doing express what I really am inside?" and: "How am I building up the other person's idea of himself?"

and: "How can I help this other person reach his potential as a child of God?" Obviously, these aren't easy questions. You have to answer them for yourself. No one else can.

Disciplined sexuality means being aware all the time of what we're doing with what we are and what we've got. It's not completely possible, of course, but it's the only goal worth shooting for. So it makes a difference about what you wear and how you wear it, what you say and how you say it, which jokes you tell and why you tell them, why you dance and how you do it.

Does what's going on tend to divide or unite you with other human beings? Does it focus on self or others? Does it bring loneliness or fellowship? Does it imprison or free? Is it honest? Is it of God?

The discipline is yours. You're His disciple, but He puts His disciples "on their own" with His love. No one else can be you. There are other disciples around—younger, older, and the same age—willing to share their discipleship and suggestions and views. But for the decisions in your life, you're it.

THREE FINAL THOUGHTS

Love that springs from faith and encompasses our whole being, our total person, enables us through God's grace to discern our sexual role in life and decide how to live it. For we believe:

1. *God treats us honestly.*
He created sexuality and calls us to live fully and freely as sexual beings.

We can thwart His desire and misuse His gift. But God is greater and stronger than sin or the conscience that accuses us.

"His orders are that we should put our trust in the name of His Son, Jesus Christ, and love one another"—that's a direct quote from His Word. (1 John 3:23)

He will not leave us alone to struggle with our sexuality.

2. *Faith is a force in our lives.*
Faith is not merely knowledge or information. It
absorbs God's power, His grace that enables us to live
differently, to love differently, in reflection of the
way He loves us.

To believe means to know that the old era has passed
away. *Everything*—but *everything*—is fresh and
new. By His death and resurrection Christ has reconciled
the entire creation to God. He's still in charge of
everything. Personal, chemical, and technological
chain reactions are in His hand. Sexual attraction,
desire, and love are under His rule.

What remains is for us to be and continually to become
what we already are: female and male, women and men,
lover and loved one, girl and fellow, belonging to
Christ and living fully in Him.

3. *God's Spirit won't give up!*
The power of God is on tap and working among us
before we even think to ask. The Spirit keeps
calling back the power of our Holy Baptism. The
fresh water and refreshing Word join to convince
us daily that it's really possible to be dead to sin
and alive to God.

The Spirit keeps us coming back to the Holy Supper
and renews us through Christ's real presence with
the bread and the wine. He keeps us celebrating the
truth that God still cares and the fact that He's at
work among us right now.

The Spirit makes God's Word more than a book.
He keeps it sharp to cut through to the heart of
everything. He keeps it alive and powerful and
moving in and through people.

The Spirit blesses us . . . and keeps us!

IT ISN'T EASY, FATHER

It isn't easy, Father,
*   to know about sex*
*   and to be sexual,*
*   to be free and open and accepting*
*   and to be aware of You and Your presence,*
*   to want to love*
*   and to want to be loved,*
*   to seek to know the mystery*
*   and to never want the mystery to end.*
*   And in the middle of it all*
*   to know You and Your love more deeply*
*   when I can't even figure out myself or any love.*

It isn't easy, Father.
*   Remind me, Lord,*
*   that no one said it would be easy.*   *prayer*
*   Teach me, Lord,*
*   the difference Your real presence makes.*
*   Show me, Lord,*
*   the power and possibility of my body,*
*   my mind, and my spirit*
*   knotted with Your overwhelming love.*

It isn't easy, Father,
*   to be fully human, like Your Son,*
*   and really God's, like Your Son,*
*   At the same time.*
*   Wake me again, Father,*
*   and tie me up with Him,*
*   with His death and life,*
*   with all death and life,*
*   with my death and life,*
*   so I can be human*
*   and can be Yours.*

Wake me again, Father.

WORDS, WORDS, WORDS

ADULTERY	Voluntary, illicit sexual intercourse between a married person and a person of the opposite sex who is not the lawful spouse.
CHASTITY	A quality of the spirit entailing deep respect and profound value for human relationships.
CLITORIS	A small projection of tissue in front of the vagina; becomes erect when stimulated.
COITUS	The act of sexual intercourse, penetration of the vagina by the penis with emission of seminal fluid.
CONTRACEP-TIVE	A device, chemical, or pill to prevent conception.
EXTRAMARITAL	Literally "outside marriage," implying adulterous sexual intercourse or intercourse between unmarried persons.
FEMALENESS	The composite of features, appearance, attributes, feelings, and outlook—some natural and some acquired—generally considered typical and desirable for the female human being. These often vary in different cultures.
FORNICATION	Illicit sexual intercourse on the part of an unmarried person.
FREE LOVE	Sexual experience without any moral limitation.
GENITALS	The organs of reproduction; especially the external sexual organs: vagina and clitoris in females; penis and testicles in males.
GOING ALL THE WAY	In this book: sexual intercourse or mutual masturbation to orgasm outside of marriage.
HOMOSEXUALITY	1. Sexual desire or love for one of the same sex. 2. The state of loving one's own, not the opposite sex.
LOVE	An attitude of the will as well as of the heart—

definitions

	a desire for the loved one, plus a desire to be united and identified with the loved one in mutual response.
LUST	Principle of self-gratification with reference to sex. "I want for myself."
MALENESS	The composite of features, appearance, attributes, feelings, and outlook — some natural and some acquired — generally considered typical and desirable for the male human being. These often vary in different cultures.
MARRIAGE	In our society, a public, mutually accepted, and lifelong commitment of a man and a woman to each other; includes the full use and enjoyment of sex.
MASTURBATION	Manual stimulation of one's own sexual organs to produce relief of sexual tension.
MATURITY	The growing ability to combine the satisfaction of instinctive drives with willing acceptance of frustration.
MENSTRUATION	The "monthly" flow of blood lasting 1 to 7 days in women between the ages of approximately 12 and 50.
NECKING	Sex play, involving kissing and hugging; mostly activity "from the neck up."
ORGASM	The climax of the sexual act; an intensely pleasurable experience for female and male, accompanying seminal emission by the male.
PENIS	The male organ of joining in sexual intercourse.
PETTING	Sex play, mostly activity "from the neck down"; "everything but" sexual intercourse.
PREMARITAL	Literally, "before marriage," referring to sexual intercourse before the persons are married.
PROMISCUITY	Mixed, disordered condition; commonly used

for casual and unrestricted sexual relations.

RELATIONSHIP   Involvement of persons, motivated and maintained by love.

SEX   Contrasted to sexuality: the instinctive drive that attracts persons of opposite sexes and insures the continuation of the species.

SEXUAL INTERCOURSE   Penetration of the vagina by the penis with the emission of seminal fluid by the male; coitus.

SEXUALITY   A function of relationship between two persons—the dynamic force of human beings which enables the personality to attain its goal—to exist for others, to love. Ability to attract and respond to another in a way in which each is changed.

VAGINA   The female sexual organ which receives the penis.

VENEREAL DISEASE   An infection transmitted through sexual intercourse, such as syphilis and gonorrhea; popularly known as VD.

VULVA   The external female sex organs surrounding the genital opening.

sons—the dynamic force of human beings which enables the personality to attain its goal—to exist for others, to love. Ability to attract and respond to another in a way in which each is changed.

VAGINA The female sexual organ which receives the penis.

VENEREAL DISEASE An infection transmitted through sexual intercourse, such as syphilis and gonorrhea; popularly known as VD.

VULVA The external female sex organs surrounding the genital opening.

READ ON

POPULAR READING

Bash, Ewald. *Christianity in Particular.* Minneapolis: Division of Youth Activity, The American Lutheran Church, 1962.

—————. *Love and Sexuality: A Place to Walk.* Minneapolis: Division of Youth Activity, The American Lutheran Church, 1966.

Bracher, Marjory L. *Love, Sex, and Life.* Philadelphia: Fortress Press, 1964.

Davis, Maxine. *Sex and the Adolescent.* New York: Permabooks, 1960.

Duvall, Evelyn Millis. *Love and the Facts of Life.* New York: Association Press, 1963.

Habel, Norman C. *Wait a Minute, Moses!* St. Louis: Concordia Publishing House, 1965.

Heuvel, Albert H. van den. *These Rebellious Powers.* New York: Friendship Press, 1965.

Hulme, William E. *Youth Considers Sex.* New York: Thomas Nelson & Sons, 1965.

Landers Ann. *Ann Landers Talks to Teen-Agers about Sex.* New York: Crest Book, 1965.

Marty, Martin E. *The Hidden Discipline.* St. Louis: Concordia Publishing House, 1962.

Miller, Randolph Crump. *Youth Considers Parents as People.* New York: Thomas Nelson & Sons, 1965.

Phillips, J. B. *Making Men Whole.* New York: Macmillan Co., 1953.

Quoist, Michel. *Prayers.* New York: Sheed & Ward, 1963.

Sauer, Chuck. *Heading for the Center of the Universe.* St. Louis: Concordia Publishing House, 1965.

Weir, Frank E. *Sex and the Whole Person.* Nashville: Abingdon Press, 1962.

ADVANCED READING

Grimm, Robert. *Love and Sexuality.* New York: Association Press, 1964.

books

Hulme, William E. *God, Sex, and Youth*. Englewood Cliffs, N. J.: Prentice-Hall, Inc., 1959.

Mead, Margaret. *Male and Female*. New York: William Morrow and Co., Inc., 1949.

Robinson, John A. T. *Christian Morals Today*. Philadelphia: Westminster Press, 1964.

Shinn, Roger Lincoln. *Tangled World*. New York: Charles Scribner's Sons, 1965.

Wynn, John C., ed. *Sex, Family, and Society*. New York: Association Press, 1966.

SPECIALIZED READING

Bailey, Sherwin. *Sexual Ethics*. New York: Macmillan Paperbacks, 1962.

Bovet, Theodor. *A Handbook to Marriage*. Garden City, N. Y.: Doubleday & Co., Inc., 1960.

Cole, William Graham. *Sex and Love in the Bible*. New York: Association Press, 1959.

Dicks, Russell L. *Premarital Guidance*. Englewood Cliffs, N. J.: Prentice-Hall, Inc., 1963.

Feucht, Oscar E., ed. *Sex and the Church*. St. Louis: Concordia Publishing House, 1961.

Friedan, Betty. *The Feminine Mystique*. New York: W. W. Norton & Co., Inc., 1963.

Hansen, Paul G., and others. *Engagement and Marriage*. St. Louis: Concordia Publishing House, 1959.

Hefner, Hugh M. *The Playboy Philosophy*, Parts I, II, III. Chicago: HMH Publishing Co., 1962–64.

Kuhn, Donald. *The Church and the Homosexual*. San Francisco: Glide Urban Center, 1964.

Piper, Otto A. *The Biblical View of Sex and Marriage*. New York: Charles Scribner's Sons, 1960.

Thielicke, Helmut. *The Ethics of Sex,* trans. John W. Doberstein. New York: Harper & Row, 1964.

NOTES

1. *The American Sex Revolution* (Boston: Porter Sargent Publisher, 1956), pp. 17–18.
2. "Sex Education Comes of Age," *Look,* XXX (March 8, 1966), 22.
3. "A Brothel in Noble Dimensions: Today's Sexual Mores" in *Sex, Family, and Society,* ed. John Charles Wynn (New York: Association Press, 1966), p. 46.
4. *Christian Morals Today* (Philadelphia: Westminster Press, 1964), p. 45.
5. "Toward a New Sexual Morality?" *The Catholic World,* CCII (October 1965), 15.
6. William E. Hulme, *Youth Considers Sex* (New York: Thomas Nelson & Sons, 1965), p. 40.
7. *Towards a Quaker View of Sex* (London: Friends Home Service Committee, 1962), p. 18.
8. Hulme, p. 43.
9. "Slang words for sexual attraction and for a variety of sexual acts, positions, and relationships are more common than standard words. Standard non-taboo words referring to sex are so scarce or remote and scientific that slang is often used in referring to the most romantic, the most obscene, and the most humorous sexual situations. Slang is . . . universally used in sexual communication . . . ." (Stuart Berg Flexner in the Preface to Harold Wentworth and Stuart Berg Flexner *Dictionary of American Slang* [New York: Thomas Y. Crowell Co., 1960], p. xiii.)
10. Donald M. MacKinnon and others, *God, Sex, and War* (Philadelphia: Westminster Press, 1965), p. 96.
11. Robert Grimm, *Love and Sexuality,* trans. David R. Mace (New York: Association Press, 1964), p. 120.
12. Paul G. Hansen and others, *Engagement and Marriage* (St. Louis: Concordia Publishing House, 1959), p. 159.
13. See Grimm, p. 119.
14. Grimm, p. 79.

15. Marjory L. Bracher, *Love, Sex, and Life* (Philadelphia: Fortress Press, 1964), p. 50.
16. Evelyn Millis Duvall, *Love and the Facts of Life* (New York: Association Press, 1963), p. 200.
17. Bracher, p. 67.
18. Maxinne Davis, *Sex and the Adolescent* (New York: Permabooks, 1960), p. 143.
19. Davis, p. 143.
20. Ann Landers, *Ann Landers Talks to Teen-agers about Sex* (New York: Crest Book, 1965), p. 41.
21. Landers, p. 27.
22. Duvall, pp. 53–57.
23. Bracher, p. 80.
24. Ewald Bash, *Love and Sexuality: A Place to Walk* (Minneapolis: Division of Youth Activity, The American Lutheran Church, 1966), pp. 46–51.
25. See Randolph Crump Miller, *Youth Considers Parents as People* (New York: Thomas Nelson & Sons, 1965), pp. 21–23.

Typefaces: Century Schoolbook, Helvetica, Palatino, and Domino

Paper: Millbrook Offset
Andorra Cover

Graphics: Ken Paul

Typefaces: Century Schoolbook, Helvetica,
          Palatino, and Domino
Paper: Millbrook Offset
           White Textcover — Homespun Embossed
Graphics: Ken Paul